Break me,
Shape me

Break me, Shape me

Working out commitment in the real world

ROB FROST

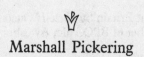

Marshall Pickering

Marshall Morgan and Scott
Marshall Pickering
Middlesex House, 34–42 Cleveland Street,
London W1P 5FB, U.K.

First published in 1986 by Marshall Morgan and Scott
Publications Ltd
Part of the Marshall Pickering Holdings Group
Reprinted 1989

British Library Cataloguing in Publication Data

Frost, Rob
    Break me, shape me: working out commitment in
    the real world.
    1. Evangelistic work
    I. Title
    269'.2'0924   BV3790

    ISBN 0–551–01326–5

Text set in Linotron Plantin by Input Typesetting Ltd,
London
Printed in Great Britain by Hazell Watson & Viney
Limited, Member of BPCC plc, Aylesbury, Bucks,
England

To 'Boss'

Contents

Introduction

It's great to tell people about Jesus!

Over the last few years I've been working as an evangelist, and I've really enjoyed it! I've been talking about Jesus in all kinds of strange places. I've invited people to follow Jesus Christ when I've spoken in plush theatres or prisons, on street corners or in television studios.

I believe that Jesus Christ is God's Son, and that through His death on the cross He saves us from sin. I believe that as we put our faith in Him and receive Him into our lives as Lord and Saviour He gives us a new start. I really want others to know Jesus as I know Him.

There's nothing better than leading someone to Christ! When I hear someone pray their first prayer of commitment I want to shout 'Hallelujah' . . . and sometimes I do! For I know that I have found a new Christian brother or sister!

But what next? After the emotion and joy of that first prayer has worn off how do we work out that commitment in everyday life?

Being a Christian in these last years of the twentieth century isn't easy. The cost of commitment is great. The question is, are we willing to pay the price?

1: Meet The Potter

I was bored and fed up with church life when I was a teenager. I preferred to ride my bike around the park than be in Sunday school. I had been dragged along to church since my earliest childhood days, and I'd had about as much as I could take.

My cherished memories of Sunday school were of the pranks I played rather than the lessons I learned. I remember being expelled from my primary class for mucking up the Lord's prayer; and I got into trouble in the Senior group for tying a girl's pony-tail to the chair back.

I knew everything *about* Christianity by my mid-teens, but I hadn't met the Saviour. I had been to so many church meetings that I knew the Bible very well, but I didn't know Jesus at all.

One weekend our youth group went on a camp to the village of Alvechurch, outside Birmingham. It was there that I began to see beyond my Sunday school religion. For the first time I glimpsed the reality of the living Saviour who had died for me and who was willing to enter my life in a new and powerful way. It was a very stuttering, hesitant kind of commitment, but it was very real to me. In the quietness of the woods I prayed, 'I'm not sure if I can accept it all or believe it all, Lord . . . but I do want to follow you and I do want you to be in the centre of my life.' There, in the stillness of the forest, I met Jesus Christ. He became a real friend to me and for the first time I believed His great promise: 'I will never leave you nor forsake you.' I took Him at His word.

My relationship with Jesus Christ is at the centre of my life. There have been many times when I've failed Him and let Him down; but He has always brought me back.

At one time in my life I became aware that my relationship with Jesus was drying up. A group of friends prayed for me, and challenged me to re-discover the living relationship with Jesus I once had known. I re-committed my life to Christ, and as a constant reminder of that new commitment I stuck a large sign on my door which read: 'Tell Jesus'. Whenever I went out of the door I couldn't help but see it. Sometimes I went out of that door to face an exam. Like most students I hated exams! The nerve-racking, finger biting, adrenalin-pumping feelings that preceded each paper nearly drove me insane. But as I went out of the door the sign reminded me to 'Tell Jesus'. And as I paused and gave each new situation to Him I found new peace. Other occasions were not as dreadful. When I was rushing out to meet my girl friend (complete with best shirt and aftershave), I again saw the sign. It reminded me that I needed to share the good times with Him too. Then there were those depressing days when everything seemed to go wrong. My work would get me down and I would be full of churned up emotion. But there was the sign yet again, 'Tell Jesus'. He was ready to share even the most miserable hours.

I am sure that this is what living Christianity is all about. Hebrews 12.2 says:

> 'Let us keep our eyes fixed on Jesus, on whom our faith depends from beginning to end.'

Maintaining a living relationship with Jesus isn't easy. I can guarantee that whenever I turn to prayer the door bell rings, the phone goes or the children yell for attention. I find that I need to go out of the house and actually make an appointment to meet the Lord.

The park near my home where I go to pray is a quiet place. There's a lovely tree-lined path, a river and plenty of long green grass. Time and again I have met Jesus there. I have stopped as the reality of His presence has burst in upon me afresh and have rejoiced anew that I know the risen Saviour. Ten minutes in His presence is enough to release me from the hectic pressures of the day. I have often gone into the park wound up with worry, and left it with a new experience of His peace.

The joy of a living relationship with Jesus is one of the most precious things I have. I share my innermost feelings and thoughts with Him in traffic jams, on high speed trains, in heated committees and in the night hours when I cannot sleep. Again and again I have asked Him to surround me with His presence and He has never let me down.

Paul wrote to the Christians in the church at Colossae:

> 'Since you have accepted Christ Jesus as Lord, Live in union with Him. Keep your roots deep in Him, build your life on Him, and become stronger in your faith as you were taught.'

Sometimes I must admit that Jesus doesn't 'feel close' to me. But my relationship with Him doesn't rest on feelings, it rests on facts. It's not feelings that drive me out to seek His presence in the park . . . it's my commitment to Him. Because I am committed to Him I want to meet Him and to share my life with Him. Feelings come and go, and I do not measure my relationship with Jesus by them. I rest on facts. The fact that He has died for me, and the fact that I have received Him into my life as Lord and Saviour.

My relationship with Jesus is a 'good days', 'bad days' kind of relationship. We have the kind of friendship that grows even stronger in the difficult times. There is a root stability about my relationship with Jesus which is the base of all that I am. And the facts of His love and my commitment give it that stability.

I cannot gauge my spiritual life by feelings. They are a dangerous and unreliable indicator. In the same way, I don't gauge my marriage by feelings. I don't feel very much in love with my wife at 3am in the morning when the baby's teething and he won't stop yelling! As we stare across the room at each other my wife and I don't 'feel' very much in love. At other times, such as over a candle-lit dinner for two we do feel very much in love. But a good marriage goes on when the soft music stops playing. It involves a kind of loving based on commitment: a wholehearted kind of commitment which does not evaporate when things get difficult.

Feelings come and go, and I don't measure my relationship with Jesus by them. My commitment to Jesus is the basis of everything. My experience of Jesus doesn't depend on a series of emotional 'highs' and 'lows'. It isn't a matter of leaping from one great spiritual 'fix' to another. If I'm honest, I think my relationship with Jesus has grown most in the difficult times. My greatest glimpses of His love have come when I've been really down, and haven't known where to turn, except to Him.

The presence of Jesus surrounds me and holds me through all the varied situations of my life. Over the years I have learnt to trust Him more and more; and to lean back in 'the everlasting arms' of His love.

When I was a Sea Scout, (complete with short trousers and sailor's hat!) our troup rented an Old Thames sailing boat for a cruise across the English Channel. It was a fascinating experience discovering how to rely on the wind and the tide to get us to the right place at the right time!

Returning back across the Channel from Belgium we

hit a terrible storm. It lasted for twenty-four hours. I have never been so scared — or so sea sick — in my life! The deck was like a skating rink, and sheets of sea-spray crashed over us every few seconds. In order to trim the sails and move on deck we were all issued with a safety harness. We were able to move across the deck by clipping and re-clipping the harness on to safety rails along the deck. The power of the waves was tremendous, and at any moment we felt we might be swept overboard. As the storm continued I became more and more reliant on that safety harness. My life depended on it. Even when the water hit me I could lean back and feel it taking my weight. I developed a very strong sense of trust in that short piece of wire.

My trust in the Lord Jesus Christ has developed throughout my life in much the same way. When I've known times of personal loss, disappointment or worry I have learned to put my weight on to Jesus, and to discover in Him the kind of friend who is always there no matter what I'm facing. I need to get alone with Him to strengthen and renew our relationship. Over the years there have been many special times when I have sensed Him specially close to me.

One morning I walked past Whitby Abbey and down the hundred and ninety-nine steps to the old town below. Everything was still, it was too early for the tourists! The narrow streets were empty and deserted save for the clatter of a distant milk-float. I paused to look in the tiny shop-windows. I was in no hurry, the morning was mine. I ambled down the cobbled streets feeling that it was good to be alive. As I crossed the harbour bridge I paused and looked out to sea. In the distance there was a line of small fishing boats chugging out of the morning mist towards me. Seagulls wheeled above them hoping for a share of the catch. It was a beautiful sight.

It was one of those timeless mornings. No pressure, no rush, no impending deadlines. The air of calm and stillness enveloped me. I was aware that Jesus was with me. I drank in the sights and sounds of that peaceful morning scene and praised Him for all His goodness.

Within a few minutes the boats were moored alongside the quay and there was a hum of activity. A squeaky crane was hauling crates of dripping fish from the decks of the laden boats. The noise of engines throbbing and the babble of the fishermen's conversation filled the air.

I noticed a larger boat moored beside the quay. As I moved closer I noticed a group of fishermen bending low over their nets. Slowly but surely they were dragging the huge trawl net across the deck. Whenever they found a tear they took some orange twine and repaired it. As I stood and watched my mind raced back to that scene by the Sea of Galilee. I remembered James and John and Peter, and the Lord Jesus Christ striding along the sea-shore toward them. As I watched the fishermen mending their nets I marvelled that the reality of His presence has not dimmed in two thousand years. The Jesus who walked by Galilee was walking with me that morning; and the Jesus who had called those Galilean fishermen to follow Him had called me, too.

Jesus Christ is as real and alive today as He ever has been. His power and His love can be known today in as real a way as when He walked the dusty lanes of Galilee.

The Jesus who reached out and healed lepers can still heal today. The Jesus who spoke words of forgiveness to the prostitute still forgives today. The Jesus who gave the crooked tax collector a new beginning still offers us a new start now. The Jesus who mended the broken lives of the outcasts of His generation can mend us, too.

When we hand our lives over to Him we need not be scared or apprehensive. For He is the Servant King. The One who washed the disciples' feet, who poured wine and broke bread saying, 'This is my body broken for you', He is the One who died on a cross because He loved us.

14

We can hand our lumpy, malformed, unworkable slabs of humanity over to Him with complete confidence! He is the Master Potter. He sees our full potential and gives us the grace to develop our hidden possibilities. He is the One who makes disfigured lives beautiful. Christ is the Potter, we are the clay. If we are ever to reach our full potential we must immerse ourselves in His will and link our earthly lives to His transforming power. His hands are the hands that hold the world in place, and they are the hands that can hold us, too.

What good can we achieve without the loving touch of the Potter shaping and reshaping our lives? He is the One who mends broken hearts and who brings order out of chaotic situations. He has the resources to put our lives together again when they've completely fallen apart. Christ is the Potter, we are the clay. As long as a lump of clay sits in the store-room it will remain shapeless and useless. But after it has been placed in the hands of the Potter it will take on shape, form and purpose.

Jesus is available to all of us, all the time. His capacity for understanding and His resources for making us whole are limitless. I saw a dramatic demonstration of this after a televised service on Palm Sunday in 1982.

I finished my sermon with an invitation to the unseen television audience to 'phone in if they needed prayer. I peered straight into the camera lens, aware even as I spoke that there were hundreds of thousands of people listening to me that very moment. It was a bizarre sensation. I made my way past the microphones, cables and piles of equipment and out into the bright morning sunlight. The church grounds were buzzing with activity as the outside broadcast crew began the de-rig. A car pulled up and I got in.

We drove to the 'phone-in headquarters about a mile away. It was a large office complex lent to us by a local newspaper. As I pushed open the large glass door I could see that it was already a hive of activity. All thirty-six 'phones were ringing and the switchboard was full!

The counsellors sat in rows in the tiny 'phone booths. Headphones on . . . Bibles open . . . they were all engaged in conversation with people who had responded to my invitation. I moved from booth to booth and listened to the counsellors sharing their faith. Some of the callers were speaking from a few streets away in South London. Others were calling from the Channel Isles, Scotland and Southern Ireland. That great unseen audience was talking back to us.

Many of the callers were facing tremendous problems. Some had been bereaved and were saying that life without their partner somehow seemed so empty. They wanted prayer, and the assurance that Jesus was with them. Others spoke of broken relationships; of marriages that had fallen apart or of conflict with members of the family. Some felt rejected and others knew bitter division with their parents or with their children. They wanted to know the reconciling power of Jesus. There were many callers who felt lonely. They spoke of dreary days when no-one called. They wanted to know if Jesus could be with them and if He could give them strength.

I was proud of the counsellors. They sat listening for hours with unflappable patience and love. They weren't offering quick-fire solutions or shallow remedies. They were offering Jesus, a real friend.

Over five hundred people called in during those four hectic hours. At the close of every conversation the counsellor offered to pray. They were not offering a 'denomination' or an 'ecclesiastical organization', they were introducing callers to a personal Friend. Nearly three years after that programme, I have just heard of a lady who is being baptised in a Midlands church as a direct result of her 'phone call. She met Jesus Christ that Palm Sunday after 'phoning in.

This personal friendship with Jesus is the heart of all

16

true Christian faith and experience. Sometimes I hear religious people mocking this kind of relationship. I've heard them say 'I've got beyond that kind of thing.' But do they know what have they lost? For what is Christianity without a living relationship with Jesus Christ?

It is easy for us to lose the reality of His presence. Life gets so busy, and there are so many demands on our time. But maintaining a living daily relationship with Jesus through prayer, Bible study and fellowship with Him must be a priority for every Christian.

Meet the Potter. He is the One who said, 'I will never leave you nor forsake you', the One to whom you can give your life with complete confidence. For He is the One who holds the universe together, and who holds our lives in His hands.

2: Clay

I parked the car in the hospital car park and helped my pregnant wife out of the passenger seat. We walked up the stone steps and into the reception area. It was after midnight and our footsteps echoed round the empty hallway. We stepped toward the door marked 'maternity' and went through. A long winding corridor lay in front of us. It was like a tunnel and long tubular lights cast a harsh, unfriendly glare along the green walls. There was a strong smell of disinfectant and somewhere in the distance doors banged, trolleys rattled and I heard the whisper of hushed voices behind closed doors.

My wife, who was about to give birth to our first child, hobbled along slowly. I did my best to support her. The walk seemed to last for ever. At last we reached a large green door and arrived at the maternity suite. A team of smartly dressed nurses hovered around us. They spoke to each other in short clipped phrases and gave us reassuring smiles.

The machinery shocked me. After all, we had come for the birth of a baby, not the servicing of a motor car. Needles flickered, lights flashed . . . and the room echoed with the amplified beat of the unborn baby's heart. Then the sound of the heartbeat changed, an alarm sounded . . . and the room was filled with masked figures shouting orders to each other in medical terminology. It was all so unreal. We were in the twilight zone between life and death.

Suddenly with a scream and a gasp the baby was born. A boy! Our most mystical moment was ruined for ever by a giggling nurse who exclaimed, 'He shot out like a flying torpedo!'. And there, unbelievably, nestling in my arms was my new-born son. He seemed so vulnerable, so delicate and so fragile. A tiny bundle of wriggling humanity. I held his tiny hand in mine.

The masked army left us with short farewells and we were alone. My wife and I looked at each other and at our son, and marvelled at God's gift of new life. We thanked the Lord for little Andrew. It was a precious moment, and one which I will remember for the rest of my life.

A few months later I parked my car again in the same car park, climbed the same stone steps and walked through the same empty hall-way. Again, it was well after midnight. I stepped into the large rattling lift and went up to the fourth floor. The creaking doors rolled apart and I walked down the corridor towards the ward.

I opened the doors and looked inside. Everything was quiet in the darkened ward. The dim night light revealed a long row of beds on either side. There was an air of stillness. The patients were all asleep. A nurse came to the door and welcomed me. 'You're the minister? We've been expecting you. Follow me.'

She led me into a small ante-room. I was suddenly dazzled by the harsh fluorescent lighting. Then I saw her. She was lying unconscious, her head propped up on pillows. Her husband, who was sitting on the bed holding her hand, looked grey and weary. He greeted me with a glance of recognition. 'I'm glad you could come', he whispered.

We sat, hour after hour through the night, each of us holding one of her hands. Occasionally we exchanged words and glances as if to reassure each other. The patient lay quite still, except for the shallow and laboured breathing. The nurse brought tea and assured us it wouldn't be long. I prayed aloud and read the twenty-third psalm. I then prayed in the silence of my mind. I offered the whole situation to the Lord and confessed my own feeling of inadequacy to share it. The breathing gradually grew worse, it became even more irregular and difficult. It was a haunting sound in the silence of the night. I sensed a tingling pang of fear as I became aware that death was near.

Then, without any drama or struggle, her breathing stopped. There was an intensity of silence. The patient was dead — and there we were still holding her hands, and feeling awkward. I prayed, committing the lady into God's care and keeping and walked back to the lift with the bereaved husband leaning heavily on my arm. Down in the lift, across the echoing hall-way, down the stone steps and out into the night. Numbed by shock, and overawed by the sense of mystery which always accompanies death, we walked in silence to the car. I drove the man home. As I drove, the wonder of life and death and the pain of goodbyes filled my mind.

Those two nights in the hospital became closely associated in my thinking. I had held the tiny hand of my new born son and I had held the hand of a dying friend. I had shared in the mystery of life and death. These two events threw into focus for me the words of Ecclesiastes:

'We leave this world just as we entered it — with nothing.'

In the emptiness of the baby's hand and the emptiness of the dying lady's hand I saw the stupidity of much of our earthly struggle. I saw again the futility of my own desire to 'possess more and more'. The foolishness of my own struggle to 'make my mark', to 'achieve' or 'make progress'. As I watched the struggle of birth and death I realised again that I was nothing more than clay.

I believe that this is the starting point for commitment to Christ. Until we realise that our dependency must be on Him, and Him alone — we have not discovered the basis for discipleship. We are just fragile human beings.

20

Mere mortals, here on earth for a short space of time. We are flesh and blood and one day we will return to dust. We all came into the world with empty hands, and that's the way we will all leave it.

The basis of commitment to Jesus Christ is that we are the clay and He is the Potter. We are mortal, He is immortal. We are temporal, He is eternal. We are finite, He is infinite. We are limited, He is limitless. We are nothing, He is everything. We are human, He is God!

This was reinforced for me by another incident, soon after the death of my friend. Another very elderly lady died and in her will she requested that I scatter her remains around the gardens of the church. So I went to the crematorium to collect her ashes.

Behind the plush chapel there was a white tiled cremation unit, and a smiling man in overalls. 'Here you are,' he said as he handed me a plastic bag full of ash. 'Please sign for them on your way out.' Concerned that the polythene bag was about to split, he provided me with a Marks and Spencer carrier bag to put them in.

I walked around the grounds of the church in as dignified way as I could manage, scattering the contents of my Marks and Spencer bag behind me. Here was reality . . . the dust of humanity. And as the ash ran through my fingers I sensed the wonder that God had made me out of such dust as this.

We read in Genesis,

'The Lord God took some soil from the ground and formed a man out of it, he breathed life-giving breath into his nostrils and the man began to live.'

Life is God's gift. We can never manufacture it. We may tamper with the processes. But there is always a beginning and an end — and that is with the Lord, not with us. I had been a Christian for several years before the enormity of this truth dawned on me. I remember

lying on the floor of my college room in absolute broken-
ness before the Lord. I recognised before Him that I
was utterly and completely dependent on Him, and Him
alone. I confessed that I was nothing more than clay. I
offered everything I was, and everything I hoped to
become . . . and cast myself completely upon His love.

This kind of experience is totally against the spirit of
the age in which we live. From our earliest schooldays
we are taught to wonder at man's greatness and to
worship man's great technological achievements. This is
only half true! For while man has achieved much he is
still only mortal, fragile, flesh and blood. Whatever he
may achieve here on earth he still arrives — and leaves
— with empty hands!

The start of full commitment must be the offering of
our lives to God like raw lumps of clay. Recognising that
we are weak and that He is strong, and that He is the
Potter and we are just clay.

I remember as a child staying on holiday in a tiny
Cotswold village called Hook Norton. Occasionally my
cousins and I would go out into the fields to find clay.
In one field there was a marshy pool and a clay-filled
bank. I enjoyed stripping away the grass and digging out
the clay with my bare hands. We used to hack out great
lumps of clay and wrap it in newspaper. We proudly
carried it back to the farm and put it on the kitchen
table. We formed simple shapes out of it and my aunt
would 'fire' them in the old coke oven. The raw clay was
changed into simple ornaments which later we painted.

Every new Christian is like that raw clay: useless and
shapeless . . . such a mess! Yet in the hands of the Potter
. . . so full of potential! But to be clay in the Potter's
hands demands total resignation to His will. We need to
be pliable!

I don't see this quality of commitment very often
today. There are too many churchgoers who want the

blessings that Jesus offers but are unwilling to pay the price for them.

Jesus not only gives us joy, peace, love and purpose. He gives us direction. He also makes demands. He calls for sacrifice. He commands us to leave self behind. There is a cost involved in Christian descipleship, and few Christians are willing to pay it.

Becoming a Christian isn't like joining a club or a society. It's not just a matter of paying a membership fee and occasionally attending meetings. We need to offer the whole of our being to Him. Yet sadly many Christians prefer to dance the world's dervish dances of ambition, consumerism, and self-centredness, preferring the way of the world to God's way.

The symptoms of this lack of commitment are easy to see. They are evident wherever Christians are living selfish lives, achieving purely personal goals and fulfilling private ambitions, wherever Christians are missing the purpose He intended:

— When I asked one girl if she would teach a Sunday school class she offered 'occasional dates' to suit her diary. Commitment to Jesus is not governed by social engagements.

— When visiting a large college recently I heard of Christians who were sleeping around. They told me that they had found Christian morality in their situation 'unworkable'. Commitment to Jesus has never been simple.

— When I asked a crowd of young Christians to help us clean up the church they didn't show up. They had 'better things to do' that Saturday. Commitment means not turning away from hard graft.

— When I asked some leading church members why they'd not been to worship they told me they were 'out exploring with their new caravan'. Commitment to Jesus involves discipline!

— When I counselled a Christian businessman he told me that his hunger for company 'incentives' had blunted his Christian conscience. Commitment to Jesus will lead us into difficult decisions at work.

Offering your life to the Lord to be 'clay in the potter's hand' is the first and most important thing to understand about commitment. The clay cannot say to the Potter, 'You can mould me, but I'll tell you what I will become'. The clay must be totally resigned to the Potter's will.

Why is it that so many Christians have entered God's family without learning the cost of submission to Christ? Why is it that so few Christians are really willing to go anywhere, do anything or become anything that He asks? Why are so few Christians really like clay in the Potter's hand?

We can never make anything out of ourselves which has any shape, any beauty, any form or any purpose unless we place our lives in His hands. We may struggle and strain. We may work and exhaust ourselves in the heat of our effort, but we will end up with disfigured lives. We can only discover the purpose of our being, only reach our full potential and only become what the Potter intended when we offer ourselves like clay in His hands.

This quality of submission is costly. Jesus found it to be so. In the Garden of Gethsemane, knowing that His death was near, He knelt down and prayed, 'Father, if you will, take this cup of suffering away from me. Not my will, however, but your will be done.' In great anguish He continued to pray until the sweat fell from His brow like great drops of blood. It is this quality of submission which is the hallmark of true Christian commitment.

Remember we entered this world with nothing — and that is how we will leave it. We owe everything we have and everything we are to the One who gave us life. By offering back to Him the brief lives we have on earth we will discover the purpose of our being and realise the potential within ourselves that only He can see.

3: The Potter's Wheel

I have a friend who is a minister in a small Yorkshire village. He is quite a keen artist, and sometimes uses art to communicate his faith. One Sunday he told the congregation to bring to church all the rubbish they could find. They turned up with all kinds of scrap paper, empty boxes, and trash. They must have thought he was mad! Over the following days he met with several of the church members in an art workshop. The art group sorted out the rubbish and worked hard to mould it into something beautiful. When the congregation arrived the following Sunday they found their rubbish transformed into a beautiful scene depicting the cross.

In his sermon my friend used this powerful illustration to explain that through the power of the cross, Jesus is able to take our twisted and sinful lives and transform them. He takes people who feel useless and worthless and makes them whole.

I saw the Lord do this in a very wonderful way when I had only been a minister for a few months. It started when I found a crumpled letter on the mat in the front porch of our village church. I didn't know how long it had been there.

The address read simply 'The Chapel', and as there was no letter box at the church the postman had pushed it under the main doors as best he could. The contents of the letter were bewildering. The writer, using prison notepaper, begged me to go to the nearby prison to see him.

I telephoned the chaplain and made an appointment to see the man. It was my first prison visit and I found

26

it quite daunting. I rang the bell beside the huge prison gate. Somewhere inside there was a rattling of keys and a banging of doors, and eventually the main gate swung open and I was let inside.

The prison chaplain arrived and greeted me with a smile. He led me through grey courtyards and on into the maze of corridors inside. As we waited for the doors of the cell-block to be unlocked I watched a crowd of prisoners walking aimlessly around the exercise yard. There was a dreary futility about their walk. They were going nowhere and it showed. Some walked together, but most walked alone. As I stood and watched I wondered why this particular prisoner wanted to see me, a stranger. The whole thing seemed bizarre.

As we walked down the dim corridors the chaplain explained that I was to hear a confession. The prisoner was on remand and had asked to speak with a local minister. The prisoner had agreed that his confession could be used in evidence, and it would be witnessed by detectives from the murder squad.

At last we reached the door of the cell. Keys rattled and the lock turned and I found myself sitting opposite the prisoner. He was motionless, holding his head in his hands. He looked up briefly and thanked me for coming. He was very distraught. I tried to be as kind as I could. Two smartly dressed men arrived and sat behind me with notebooks out and pens poised. They were detectives.

The confession started in a halting way, but soon the prisoner gained courage to tell his story. It emerged in short, sharp sentences. He was clearly a broken person. His voice never rose above a whisper, and as he began to describe the murder he had committed, he grew more upset. Suddenly he burst into uncontrollabe sobbing.

I didn't want to hear any more, I wanted to get away. I longed for him to finish. I felt close to tears myself.

Quite suddenly it was over. The notebooks were closed and the policemen left. The prisoner looked up into my face. He began to pour out a torrent of abuse about himself. His life was a mess and there was nothing he could do to make amends for his crime. He felt he had no hope and no future. Nothing I could say seemed adequate, so I bowed my head and prayed for him. I promised to visit him again.

Over the years that followed I visited him every month. I went during the long months of remand, the stressful time of the trial and then during the years of his sentence in one dingy northern prison after another. It took a long time to build up a real relationship with him, but gradually we became friends. Over the months that followed I began to see a growing spiritual hunger in him.

Then I saw the Lord do something very wonderful in his life. He found Jesus Christ as his Saviour and gave His life to the Lord. Gradually his whole personality opened up. The Lord took this man's life and began to shape it and make something new of it. It was a miraculous work of cleansing and of healing. The man was transformed as visibly as a lump of clay is formed into a beautiful vase.

Over the years that followed I looked forward to those prison visits. I was no longer visiting a broken human being, but a brother in Christ. He became a sensitive and caring Christian.

This work which I saw Christ begin in the prisoner's life is something we should all experience. Of course we haven't all been in prison, but our sin is just as real. All of our lives are spoiled in some way by the deep roots of selfishness. It is so important that we keep offering our lives back to the Lord again and again so that he can change us and renew us. This symbol of the Potter and the clay was really brought home to me during a recent visit to Central London.

I was Christmas shopping with my family in Oxford Street. I don't like shopping anyway, but amid the jostling crowds of Central London I was finding it harder than usual. While my family went to buy some decorations I escaped for a few minutes' peace and quiet. I went into an exclusive department store and took the escalator down into a different world. The warm air enveloped me. It was good to be away from the crowds.

The china department was quiet, thickly carpeted and beautifully laid out. Spotlighted dinner services, shelves full of delicate china, figurines on pedestals, I looked at a few of the price tags: everything was out of my range.

But there, in the middle of the department, was a potter. In his working clothes, he looked out of place in that sumptuous setting. He was stooping over the wheel, his foot pressing the pedal. He was quite engrossed in his work and his gaze was fixed on the clay. His hands were covered in clay.

A giggling group of shop-girls enjoying their lunch break meandered into the department. They stood watching him, then one of the girls asked if she could try. His concentration was broken, but he didn't seem to mind. She stepped over to the wheel and took the clay in her hands. For just a moment I thought that she was going to make something good. The pot began to rise and she shaped it carefully. But suddenly it collapsed. The clay fell off the wheel and crumpled on the floor beside her. Her clothes were spattered with mud. She was annoyed. The other girls pulled her away. Their voices faded as they sauntered out of the department.

I was just about to leave, but then I noticed the potter looking at the lump of clay on the floor. He bent down and patiently placed it back on the wheel. He set the wheel spinning, and in his eyes I could see the vision of what it would become. His fingers moved gently over the spinning mass, moulding, shaping, forming. The clay slowly took a new shape. The wheel stopped. He had made a beautiful vase. He paused and looked at it, and placed it on the table beside him. It was perfect.

It reminded me of that incident recorded in the book of Jeremiah. The Lord told the young prophet to go and watch a potter at work. As he watched, the potter took a mis-shapen lump of clay and began to re-work it. The potter took something which was a mess and made it beautiful.

The Lord spoke powerfully to Jeremiah through this, and Jeremiah understood that the people of Israel were like that mis-shapen lump of clay, but the Lord would take them and re-shape them. The Lord said:

> 'Haven't I the right to do with you people of Israel what the potter did with the clay?'

Jeremiah's vision of the Potter is one which we all need to see. We all tend to get so bound up with our own plans, hopes and ambitions we forget that there is One who can shape our lives perfectly. The Creator who set the stars in their place and who coloured the rainbow's arch can form our lives. God, who made the world a beautiful place, can make beautiful people, too. He has the power and the resources to do for us things which are beyond our highest hopes.

How can we imagine the Lord's creative energy? A few years ago I visited Niagara Falls. The roar of the water was deafening, and the rainbows that danced in the swirling mist were indescribably beautiful.

I took a trip into the caves behind the Falls to see Niagara from behind. As I stood in that dark cavern and watched the thundering torrent rush past, I found it breathtaking, a living demonstration of the power of God.

As the guide told us of the plans to light up the Northern States with the power of that rushing water, I thought of the power of the Lord. Powerful enough to light up the whole universe, yet personal enough to light up each of our lives.

How can any of us believe that we can make a better job of our lives than the One who made us and who understands us best? How can we begin to ignore God whose strength and resources are all sufficient? He has a right to direct our lives. He *gave* us life. He knew us before we were born and has watched us with love down all the years. He knows our imperfections and understands our weaknesses. He knows us as a potter knows his clay.

We need to recognise His ability to make something wonderful out of our lives. We need to surrender ourselves to Him and to place our lives in His hands. We are the clay and He is the Potter.

When I was a student at Cliff College in Derbyshire we used to do manual work in the college grounds. The hours I spent in the garden were a good break from study, though I am no gardener! We used to talk and discuss as we worked. After all, a solid afternoon of weeding can be rather back-breaking! One day I was detailed to work with a student who I knew was very close to the Lord.

We talked about our relationship with the Lord, and I asked him how he had grown so much in the Christian life.

His answer really challenged me. He told me that every week he spent an hour alone in the college chapel. He called it his weekly 'sorting out session with the Lord'. During that hour he would lay his life open before God. He would ask the Holy Spirit to pinpoint areas that week where he had failed to live up to the Lord's standard. He would confess his failure, and claim forgiveness. He would also ask the Lord to change Him. To take those areas of his life which were wrong and to transform them.

The Lord's refining, purifying, re-creating process is

something which should be happening in all our lives
week by week.

Paul wrote to the Colossians:

> 'But now you must get rid of all these things: anger,
> passion, and hateful feelings. No insults or obscene
> talk must ever come from your lips. Do not lie to
> one another, for you have taken off the old self with
> its habits and have put on the new self. This is the
> new being which God, its Creator, is constantly
> renewing in His own image, in order to bring you
> to a full knowledge of Himself.'

If only we could see ourselves as He sees us: the walls
of prejudice that have built up; the bad habits that we
cling to; the hurt that is festering within us; evil motives
that we've whitewashed with good intentions; deep
rooted self-centredness. These are the things which the
Creator can change within us. He can take our lives like
a potter takes a mis-shapen lump of clay — and make
something beautiful. Our lives need to be constantly
renewed so that we become like Jesus.

Over the last few years I have been trying to offer my
life to the Lord in such a way that he can continue His
work within me. He has been working on my insecurity,
and teaching me to rely more on Him and less on myself.
He has given me the grace to carry problems and initiate
projects which a few years ago would have been totally
beyond me. He has used the criticism of others and the
forces of failure to humble me. He has been teaching me
to work for Him instead of working for myself. In many
other ways he has been revealing wrong attitudes within
me and pinpointing areas of selfishness. I want my life
to be firmly in the Potter's hand.

Some Christians seem to think that this offering of
their lives to the Lord need only be done once. I don't
agree. As the years go by I find that I need to come back

to the Lord again and again. As I mature as a Christian I find new areas of my life which I need to offer to Him; and I begin to see more clearly just how much I need Him.

Some of our spiritual forefathers knew what it was to give everything to the Lord. In his journal, George Whitfield described how one beautiful day in May 1737 he was strolling down a country lane. The beauty of the spring flowers and the green hedgerows made him feel good. As he walked he came very aware of the Lord's presence with him. It grew so real that he lay prostrate on the ground and offered his life to God. He wrote in his journal,

'I offered myself like a blank cheque in His hands.' It was his way of saying that he gave his life to Christ without limit or reserve. If the Potter is to transform our lives we need to offer ourselves with the same wholeheartedness.

John Wesley, writing in his journal, described the kind of peace and joy which fills our lives when we yield ourselves wholeheartedly to the Lord. Under the date Sunday, November 29th 1761 he wrote:

'We had a comfortable love feast, at which several declared the blessings they had found lately. We need not be careful by what name to call them, while the thing is beyond dispute. Many have, and many do daily experience an unspeakable change. After being deeply convinced of inbred sin, particularly of pride, anger, self-will and unbelief, in a moment they feel all faith and love; no pride, no self-will, or anger: and from that moment they have continual fellowship with God, always rejoicing, praying and giving thanks. Whoever ascribes such a change to the devil, I ascribe it to the Spirit of God: and I say, let whoever feels it wrought, cry to

God that it may continue; which it will, if he walks closely with God; otherwise it will not.'

One of the famous Wesley hymns sums it all up, it's called Huddersfield.

Come then, and dwell in me,
Spirit of power within,
And bring the glorious liberty
From sorrow, fear and sin:

The seed of sin's disease,
Spirit of health, remove,
Spirit of finished holiness,
Spirit of perfect love.

Thrice acceptable word,
I long to prove it true!
Take me into Thyself, O Lord,
By making me anew;

Me for Thy mercy sake
Out of myself remove,
Partaker of Thy nature make,
Thy holiness and love.

Hasten the joyful day
Which shall my sins consume,
When old things shall be passed away,
And all things new become.

He is the Potter, and we are the clay. Our daily offering of our lives into His hands enables Him to continue and complete the good work that He has begun in us. As I pause to place my life on the potter wheel I find it humbling to ask myself, 'What am I holding back?'

4: Anywhere

Commitment to Jesus Christ has to be worked out in practical decisions every day. Our commitment to him will effect decisions about whether we stay where we are or whether we move.

One of my college mates used to say, 'Here comes Rob, always in the wrong place at the wrong time'. He only meant it as a joke, but there was a sharp edge to what he said as well. There are many Christians, I'm sure, who are in the wrong place today. They have missed the Lord's direction for their lives and are not serving Him in the place where He wants them.

Until we take the 'ifs and buts' out of our commitment to Jesus Christ we will not be available to go where He sends. A crucial part of commitment is to say, 'Anywhere you send me Lord, I will go'. For some people that commitment will mean a move to the other side of the world. For others, it will mean staying just where they are. Whatever the result, we should all aim to be in the right place at the right time. Jesus said, 'Take my yoke and put it on you, and learn from me, because I am gentle and humble in spirit; and you will find rest. For the yoke I will give you is easy, and the load I will put on you is light.'

When I visited the Island of Sark I hired a rather decrepid horse that was yoked to an equally decrepid cart! The very elderly driver beamed at us with his one tooth, and explained that he'd only ever left the Island once — and that was on a short holiday to Guernsey. He hadn't enjoyed the experience.

Our family climbed aboard the cart for a tour of the

Island. The horse clip-clopped ahead of us and the old cart rattled and shook as we drove along the unmade roads. The friendly driver lifted my four-year-old son into the driving seat and handed over the reins to him. I was quite worried. My little boy didn't know right from left, and I was afraid we'd all end up in the ditch! When my son pulled right the horse turned right. When he pulled left the horse turned left. The blinkered horse had no idea where he was headed, he simply obeyed. He trusted the driver implicitly.

To be yoked to Christ means exactly what it says. We are blinkered, and He steers. We don't know the road ahead, but He does. We are servants, He is Master. Those Christians who do not actively seek His guidance or obey his call have not taken his 'yoke' upon them. They have not made Jesus 'Lord' of their lives. This is not discipleship. It will lead 'nowhere' fast.

This is vividly illustrated by the story of Jonah. He certainly had to learn this lesson the hard way. When God asked him to go and preach to the people of Nineveh he didn't want to go. It was a pagan city and he knew he wouldn't be welcome there.

So Jonah decided on a compromise. He agreed to uproot and travel overseas as a missionary, but he would choose the location. He preferred Tarshish, it was more his kind of place and they were more his type of people there. He reckoned he would have a good time. He set sail for Tarshish, but never stopped to think through the consequences. By stepping out of the Lord's will he would end up in the wrong place at the wrong time and would be totally ineffective.

We all know what happened next. He hit stormy weather. He got into deep water. He got rather chewed up about things. He wasn't exactly having a whale of a time! But it was there in the whale's belly that Jonah asked God to forgive Him. He offered himself totally to

36

the Lord. So God forgave Him, and eventually Jonah went to Nineveh . . . God's place for him.

It certainly wasn't an easy assignment. Perhaps it wasn't what he'd have planned for himself. But it was God's place. And because he was in the right place at the right time God blessed him.

Nineveh was a huge city, it took three days to walk through it. After walking for a day Jonah proclaimed God's message. The people believed, and everyone put on sack-cloth as a symbol of their repentance.

The time was ripe for Nineveh, and if Jonah had not gone there he would never have known it. Because of his stubbornness, Jonah nearly missed a golden opportunity to serve the Lord.

We cannot plan our own lives in the Lord's service. We cannot choose the opportunities which we think are best or the places we think are 'right'. We must actively seek God's will, and submit ourselves to it.

To be in the right place at the right time may involve us in pain or persecution. God's will for our lives does not always mean an easy time, in fact it may often lead us into very difficult situations.

This was highlighted for me when I visited a small town in Eastern Europe to meet the Christians there and work with the local minister for several weeks. It was good to be away from the tourist track, and to sample real life in that small communist town. My minister friend spoke fluent English, so he was able to act as interpreter. I talked for hours with the local Christians.

One group of Christian teenagers told me about the subtle forms of persecution that they encountered. Some found it impossible to get a grant for college because they were Christians, others talked of closed career prospects and of trouble with the authorities. I was really impressed by their strong faith, and their willingness to stay faithful to Jesus Christ whatever the cost. I wished that some of my youth group could hear them talk.

A little later I met a very elderly minister. 'The trouble is', he said, 'you have many young believers in the west . . . but I don't think that their faith is very strong. Would they still follow Jesus if they had to pay the cost that our young people pay?'

I looked at his drawn grey face and asked him if he'd ever thought of leaving that country and of coming to serve Christ in the west. He looked hurt by my suggestion and paused to think through his reply. He bent forward, and with piercing eyes said, 'What would happen to the sheep if all the shepherds ran away?' For my minister friend in the East, being in the right place meant staying just where he was. It would have been easy for him to run away to an easier political climate and to find a ministry in the west with less pressure. It can sometimes be harder to stay put for God than to go running in His service. He may ask you to stay where you are.

That's not always the case, though. One of my friends was called to take up a new life at the other end of the world. For her it meant a change of culture, climate, language and career. A whole new beginning. Her name is Linda.

One day she came to visit me at Bible College. Above the hum of conversation in the college common room I heard a young Scotsman call her name. The young lad came across and tossed a badge to her. Linda caught the badge and put it on. It bore the insignia of a famous missionary society. 'The Lord could use you overseas' he said 'why don't you go?'

That incident was part of a whole train of events which confirmed Linda's call to the mission field. A few months later I heard that she had gone to train with the missionary society whose badge she'd worn. She really asked the Lord to show her where to go, and eventually she wrote to say that she was bound for Indonesia. It was quite a dramatic change for her. She moved from

Birmingham to Indonesia. Her new home was a timber hut built on stilts and she travelled around in a canoe. Many of Linda's friends marvelled at her sense of commitment. It seemed that she would never be married — and that her whole life would be lived without a husband or a family. How wrong we were! Whilst in Indonesia Linda met a Canadian missionary and they fell in love. They are now married and have three lovely children. It's just as well that Linda was in the right place at the right time! Over the years since she left Britain I have followed Linda's progress through regular correspondence. Although she has been through many difficult times she has never wavered from her call. She still writes with a quiet assurance that she is in the right place at the right time!

My minister friend in the East discovered that God's will for his life was to stay where he was. Linda, on the other hand, left everything she knew to discover God's place for her.

Each of us, as disciples of Christ, must be willing to take on the 'yoke of obedience'. Only He knows the road ahead, and only He knows the best way for us to go. He must steer, and we must wear the yoke of obedience. Jesus said, 'If anyone wants to come with me, he must forget self, take up his cross every day, and follow me. For whoever wants to save his life will lose it, but whoever loses his life for my sake will save it. Will a person gain anything if he wins the whole world but is himself lost or defeated? Of course not!'

It was a solemn warning that Jesus gave. It must have made his disciples stop and think. Following Him would involve sacrifice, and it was time for them to start carrying the cross — the symbol of death. This statement marked a turning point in His ministry. Things were going to get tough, and He didn't want anyone to continue unless they were willing to pay the price. I wonder how many of us would have gone on with Him if we'd heard Him say that? The only sure thing He promised was a cross. I wonder how many of us are following Him today with the sure knowledge that it may cost us everything?

Discovering God's will for our lives should be a priority for all of us. Unfortunately some Christians get to a point where they are genuinely confused about which way is right for them. They really want to be in the right place at the right time, but they can't seem to discover where that place is!

One night I was driving South through France. It had been a long drive and my car-load of passengers were all sleeping peacefully. The rain was lashing onto the windscreen. It had been an awful journey. I peered through the torrential rain, and was quietly admitting to myself that I was lost. I decided that my sleeping passengers didn't need to know that. Finally, I stopped at a crossroads. The headlights picked out two large signs pointing in opposite directions. One read 'Toutes directions' and the other 'toutes autres directions'. Even my limited knowledge of French was sufficient to translate 'all directions' and 'all other directions'. I laughed in disbelief. I just didn't know where to turn. There wasn't enough information; and I sat there for some time not knowing what to do!

Life can be just as confusing! We may be faced with several alternatives at once, and it can sometimes be hard to know which way to go. One thing is for sure, only *one* way is God's way. The others will all be second best.

This sense of confusion may centre around where we should live, what kind of job we should do, or the kind of Christian service to get involved with. It may even involve whom we should marry!

I believe that the Lord speaks to us in many different ways. In my own life I have identified six different methods that God seems to use to point me in the right direction.

Sometimes he speaks supernaturally. Maybe through a prophesy, a vision, or a clear and unmistakable word which we know has come to guide us. This has only happened a couple of times in my life.

It happened for Paul after his successful missionary visits to Derbe and Lystra. He was blocked from proceeding into Asia and he was blocked from proceeding into Bithynia. So we went to Troas to wait. He must have felt frustrated and confused. His plans to take the gospel to Asia and Bithynia were ready; but for some undisclosed reason they were not to be followed through. Whilst in Troas he had a vision in which he saw a Macedonian begging him to go and preach the gospel there. As soon as Paul had seen this vision he prepared to leave for Macedonia. He followed God's call without question or hesitation. The result was the planting of the church at Philippi.

Sometimes when we come to a crossroads in life, or to some place where the future seems blocked and confused we should look for a sign from the Lord. Some indisputable word which speaks to the heart of our situation.

Secondly, I believe that the Lord speaks to us through need. It's so easy to turn a blind eye and a deaf ear to urgent needs, and to keep on seeking the Lord's will!

That need may come to us in many forms. A lonely shut-in who needs a visitor. A mission hospital short of nurses. A Sunday school which is short of teachers. A tribe without the Bible in their native language.

Jesus warned us that He would come to us in the cries of the needy. We may not recognise His presence, but one day it will be revealed to us . . .

' "When, Lord, did we ever see you hungry and feed you, or thirsty and give you drink? When did we ever see you a stranger and welcome you in our homes, or naked and clothe you? When did we ever

41

see you sick or in prison, and visit you?" The King will answer back, "I tell you, indeed, whenever you did this for one of the least important of these brothers of mine, you did it for me!" '

Thirdly, I'm sure that the Lord often uses our natural gifts and interests in His service. The Lord has rarely asked me to do anything for which I've felt unsuited. He often 'tailor makes' opportunities to fit my gifts perfectly. Paul wrote to the Corinthians . . .

'There are many different kinds of spiritual gifts, but the same Spirit gives them. There are different ways of serving, but the same Lord is served. There are different abilities to perform service, but the same God gives ability to everyone for their particular service.'

Sometimes it is hard for us to see where our strengths lie, and what particular gifts the Lord has given us for serving Him. It's good to talk this through with mature Christians, so that we can see the kind of things which God has equipped us to do.

Fourth, I believe that God speaks to us through a growing 'inner conviction' that something is right. I can't really describe it, except that I've found it to be stronger than a 'hunch', and something which may linger with me for months or even years until I respond to it. Sometimes this feeling may be telling me that something is 'right'. There is some course of action I need to follow, and something I really need to do. The conviction only disappears when I say 'yes'. But occasionally this feeling is a warning that something is wrong. I must move out of some form of ministry or activity because it is wrong. I am uneasy until I have said 'no'.

On returning home after seeing a beautiful church in the north of England where I had been invited to become minister I had this niggling sense of unease about the invitation. Everything about the church and the work there *seemed* so right, but it didn't *feel* right. But I know that hunches and feelings can sometimes prove dreadfully wrong, so I went to see some mature Christian friends who were willing to spend time with me thinking and praying about God's will. I shared my nagging doubts with them, and they confirmed my 'hunch'. I did not go.

This leads me on to the fifth point! *I believe that the Lord often uses the Church to guide us and direct us.* I have a network of older Christian friends to whom I look for guidance and advice about the course of my life and ministry. This is quite Biblical. In Galatians 6.2 we read,

> 'Help carry one another's burdens, and in this way you will obey the law of Christ.'

One young man once wrote to me in desperation. Having followed a strong 'hunch' he had launched out into a full time ministry for the Lord. But he had not tested his conviction with other Christians or submitted himself to the authority of church leaders. His letter read like a disaster from start to finish. He had become alienated from his family, his friends and his fellowship. He was in serious financial difficulty and his work was in a mess. He didn't know where to turn for help. All this might have been avoided if he had tested his 'hunch' with the people of God.

Finally, following God's call is often an active process. I don't believe that the Lord wants us to waste years of our lives in a wilderness of confusion because we're unwilling to start exploring possible ways ahead.

In my own life and ministry I keep trying doors and exploring alternatives in order to discover which way is right for me. One mature Christian once advised me,

'Follow your nose until the Lord puts it out of joint', and I've found there's a lot of truth in that.

Though I have been through times of confusion and indecision in my own life I remain convinced that God does have a purpose and a plan for me. I really do want to find it and follow it. Sometimes we only see how clearly he's guided us when we look back.

This was highlighted for me when I was talking to a great Christian man about his life. He had terminal cancer, and we both knew that he did not have long to live. As the time of his death was drawing closer he began to reflect on his life and his past. As he thought back over the years he began to think about God's guidance and the way his life had gone. 'As I look back,' he said, 'I can see signposts staked all across the years. Points of decision when out of the gloom I found God's will for me.'

I suppose it's easier to see the route with hindsight, when the journey's over. God is guiding us and showing us the way, but perhaps we'll only see how plainly when we look back across the years.

I brought back from my stay in the communist town a rough clay pot which I saw made in the potter's shop. It's a shepherd's flask, and it was given to me by my minister friend. It has always been a reminder that commitment to Christ may be costly.

For some, that cost must be paid by staying just where they are. For others, it may mean a new beginning at the other end of the world. What matters is that the Potter puts us where he wants us. Wherever that may be!

5: Anytime

It was a dark, wintry afternoon and the snow was cascading down. I was out on my rounds in the mining village where I was a minister. I had spent three hours visiting the sick and the elderly, and it was nearly time to go home. It was my last visit of the afternoon. I swallowed the strong brew of tea and placed the fragile cup and saucer on the table. I bade the frail old lady farewell and trudged through the snow to my car. I had finished my visiting list, and I was ready for a break. The roads were treacherous and the wheels on my car slithered as I drove through the snow. It was clear that we were in for a bad night.

At the end of the road I got a strong feeling that I should go and visit an elderly man: I pulled the handbrake on, leant back, and sighed. I really didn't want to bother. I sat and analysed the feeling. I wondered if I was going mad. Maybe I was overtired, or was trapped by some guilt complex. Maybe the Lord was trying to tell me something! This old man didn't really need a visit, he was quite well . . . and he surely wouldn't expect me to call on such a snowy afternoon. Several moments passed as I tried to make a decision.

At last I gave in. Instead of turning left towards home I turned right toward this man's house. By now the snow was falling in great white clumps, and the car laboured as I drove up the steep hill toward the council estate where he lived.

I went in through the gate and knocked on the back door, as is normal in mining villages. The old man greeted me warmly and put the kettle on. Soon I was consuming yet another cup of hot strong tea. We chatted for a while, and we shared our faith together. We ended with a time of prayer.

I went back home wondering why I'd been to see him. It made no sense at all! Several hours after my visit, however, the old man died of a heart attack. I was one of the last people to speak to him.

If I hadn't trusted my gut feeling and gone to visit him, I think I'd have lived the rest of my life with a tinge of regret. I am sure that the Lord guides us; and that if we're really listening to Him and sensitive to His prompting, we will be in the right place at the right time.

I try to live my life so that I am available 'anytime' for the Lord. Over the years I have realised that His call to action often comes at inconvenient moments. It has sometimes overturned my list of priorities, interrupted my social life and made me late for other important engagements. As I am pencilling in appointments in my diary, I try to sense the Lord's will for my days and hours. Yet sometimes He needs to overrule what I've written in my diary and lead me into situations I know nothing about. His will doesn't always fit neatly around our plans!

When we say 'anytime' to the Lord, it means taking the barriers down and letting Him be Lord of *all* our time. There are Christians who never realise that the Lord may have a job for them to do while they're at work, on holiday or in transit. Of course, if you want to remain ineffective in the Christian life there are always plenty of excuses. There are three simple excuses which many Christians use whenever the Lord asks them to do anything! They are 'I'm tired', 'I'm busy', and 'I'm booked up'. Let's look at them closely.

'I'm tired'

Many Christians consider themselves 'off duty' for service whenever they're tired. This means that large areas of their time are 'out of bounds' to the Lord. They regard such times as 'personal', and would not expect the Lord to ask anything of them when they're resting.

There are too many Christians working 'shop hours' in the Kingdom. They are not available to the Lord in the evenings, over the weekends or during their annual holidays. And consequently they're missing out on some of the most rewarding opportunities for service that He has in store.

The story of Philip the evangelist and the Ethiopian official really gets through to me whenever I'm feeling too tired to serve the Lord. Philip had just finished a big mission in the capital city of Samaria. There had been large crowds at the meetings, and people had been healed. The whole city had been influenced by the mission. I'm sure that both spiritually and physically he was exhausted. Mission work leaves you elated, but completely drained. Even so, an angel ordered Philip to leave town at once and go to the road linking Jerusalem and Gaza.

Without a moment's hesitation Philip went. It must have seemed a bit of a come-down, standing by some desert road after conducting such an important city-wide mission. Just then, an Ethiopian treasury official passed by in a carriage. He was reading Isaiah's description of the Suffering Servant, the prophecy about Jesus.

At once Philip saw the purpose of his journey. He began to jog alongside the chariot, and he talked to the official. Before long the two men were deep in conversation and the Ethiopian began to ask serious questions about Jesus Christ.

The rest of the story is well known. The official believed in Jesus and was baptised in a stream near the road. And it happened because a tired man went and stood by a road in the middle of no-where!

I'm sure that I've missed important opportunities for serving the Lord because I've said 'I'm too tired'. Of course, I know it is important to rest and relax . . . but I also know that I can use my tiredness as an excuse for disobedience.

I don't think we've fully grasped what Jesus meant when he told us to be like servants. It's hard for us to really understand what Jesus meant by that. After all, the servants of his time had to work much harder than any working people today. They were at their master's command every hour of every day. There were no annual holidays or long weekends. There was no time to relax or take life easy. The servant was always available.

So when we offer all our time to the Lord we are not doing something extra special. We are only doing what he expects of us! After all, Jesus said:

> 'The servant does not deserve thanks for obeying orders, does he? It is the same with you; when you have done all you have been told to do, say, "We are ordinary servants; we have only done our duty."'

Of course, this style of Christian living is very costly. Yet it opens us up to being in the centre of the Lord's will — even when we're tired! When we allow each day to be fully His we become really usable. At last we can honestly say to the Lord that we're available!

'I'm busy'

There are some teachers you never forget! When I was a teenager one of my college lecturers was a tall bearded man with an unapproachable manner. He was always reciting his favourite motto, which went, 'You have all of my sympathy, but none of my time'.

He lived by what he said. It was hard to talk to him

because he was always rushing off somewhere. I didn't want his sympathy, I wanted a few moments of his time to help me with my work. He was always too busy.

I'm sure that many of us have so filled our lives with all kinds of 'important' activities, that we're just not available to respond to the Lord's will. Day after day we rush from one place to the next, offering everyone we meet 'all of our sympathy but none of our time'.

Jesus wasn't like that. No matter how busy He was, He always had time. Jairus, that official in the local synagogue, was deeply upset. His twelve-year-old daughter was dying. He pleaded with Jesus to go and see her, it was his only hope. As Jesus was rushing to the house to see Jairus's daughter He felt someone touch the edge of His cloak. Even though He was in a great hurry, He stopped. There, in the crowd, was someone in deep need.

A woman who had suffered from severe bleeding for twelve years had reached out and touched His cloak. Jesus had time for her, and He said: 'My daughter, your faith has made you well. Go in peace.'

To many of us the woman in the crowd would have been an 'interruption'. She wasn't an interruption to Jesus, she was someone in desperate need. She had a rightful claim on His time.

When I was a student in theological college my study was cleaned by a small Austrian woman. When I was at my desk trying to write an essay or read a book she would pop in for a chat. At first I considered her visits an interruption, but gradually I began to see her as a friend. We were able to talk about Christ together, and she kept me supplied with delicious apple pies!

One day I heard that she had suffered a major heart attack, and shortly afterwards she died. I really missed her daily visit. I began to realise how much her friendship had meant to me. I thanked God for her life.

The Lord sends people into our lives for many reasons.

Yet so often we consider them as 'interruptions' to our busy schedule. We are missing out on opportunities for service.

The parable of the Good Samaritan should make us all stop and think. The Priest who passed by the injured man was thinking about his duties in the Temple. It was the same with the Levite, his mind was full of religious duties that he didn't stop to help. They were both too busy to care. It took a Samaritan, someone considered a 'second class citizen', to stop and help the wounded man. The Priest and the Levite were so busy for God that they couldn't see what He wanted them to do.

I'm sure that I've been like the Priest and the Levite. I've been so busy that I've missed seeing the real needs. Saying 'anytime' to the Lord must mean that we're available, even when we're rushed off our feet!

The very impression of feverish activity which many of us create can harm our Christian witness. One family, who had passed through a terrible crisis, called me in after the event and said, 'We didn't want to bother you at the time, you were so busy.'

We can be moving through life at such a speed that we meet people but we don't get to know them. We hear people, but don't listen to them. We look at people, but don't see their need. We miss opportunities for serving those who are all around us. We say to the Lord 'anytime, but not just now!'

'I'm booked up'

This third excuse is generally used of our long-term plans. Many of us say 'yes' to God's call, but we have other things to do first. We are sure that one day we will respond to the call, but it will be later rather than sooner.

It may be a call to teach in the Sunday school, and we say 'Yes, when I've finished my exams'. Or it could be a call to the ministry, and we say 'Yes, when I've paid off my mortgage'. Or perhaps a call to go overseas, and we say 'Wait until I'm married'.

One day the prophet Isaiah went into the Temple. He glimpsed something of the wonder and glory of the Lord. It was a powerful vision, and it made him feel helpless and inadequate. The vision ended with a question.

'Whom shall I send? Who will be our messenger?'

Isaiah, face to face with the Living God, didn't dare make excuses or ask for extra time! He declared, 'I will go. Send me.' He said 'yes' to the Lord's call. It was an immediate response.

Jesus expected his followers to answer without hesitation. There was the man who offered to follow Him after he'd attended the family funeral. It was a good excuse, but not good enough. Jesus rebuked the man with the words:

'Follow me, and let the dead bury their own dead.'

Saying 'anytime' to the Lord is a risky business. It opens us up to changed plans and unexpected opportunities. Life becomes totally unpredictable; and totally satisfying! The Lord's timing may not fit in with our career plans. It may not suit our family arrangements or our personal ambitions. But commitment is commitment is commitment, and sometimes it hurts!

This was illustrated for me in a very powerful way. I was absolutely frantic. With two weeks to go before a fifty-one town tour of the United Kingdom with the Gospel Roadshow I was an actor short. As every day passed I grew more concerned. It seemed that I wouldn't be able to find anyone suitable and get them rehearsed in time for the tour.

One day I heard about a young man with drama experience called Ray. He was out of work at the time and was therefore available. He looked like the right person. His strong commitment to Christ and his zany sense of humour made him ideal for the task! I eventually tracked him down in Morden Park, Surrey. He was strolling down a hill holding hands with a young lady. As they walked towards me they were silhouetted by the summer sun . . . it looked like a romantic television commercial.

I introduced myself and explained how desperate I was to find someone to act in the tour. Ray greeted my request enthusiastically and asked lots of questions about the purpose of the tour.

'Just a minute,' he beamed, 'what were the dates again? I can't possibly come, we're getting married mid-way through the tour. I would have enjoyed taking part but it's impossible.'

I was crestfallen. I apologised for disturbing their stroll and sauntered back to the car. It was a real disappointment, but I went home and tried to work out some other solution to the problem.

Mid-way through the evening the telephone went. It was Ray. He had postponed his wedding to take part in the Roadshow tour . . . that is, with the full permission of his fiancée Karen! When Ray said 'anytime' to the Lord he really meant it, even though it meant postponing his wedding at short notice!

We are not much use to the Lord if our future is all 'booked up'. No matter how clearly he guides us we will not be available to obey. It is so important that we offer the Lord our whole future and ask Him to guide us through it.

James wrote:

> 'Now listen to me, you that say, "Today or tomorrow we will travel to a certain city, where we will stay a year and go into business and make a lot of money." You don't even know what your life

tomorrow will be! You are like a puff of smoke, which appears for a moment and then disappears.'

James realised that our lives are in God's hands, not our own. The Lord has given us life, and he knows what is best for us. Only as we submit each decision about our future to His will can we discover the perfect plan for our lives. It is just not good enough to 'do our own thing' and hope that it may please the Lord. If we do, we'll end up in the wrong place at the wrong time!

Francis Ridley Havergal, the popular hymn writer, was a Christian for several years before she fully understood what this kind of commitment would mean. She wrote in her booklet *All for Jesus:*

'I was gratefully conscious of having loved the Lord and delighted in his service, but my experience was not up to the standard of full consecration.'

She offered her life completely to the Lord, and out of her deeper commitment flowed some of her greatest hymns. One of her most well-known ones begins:

'Take my life and let it be,
Consecrated Lord to Thee,
Take my moments and my days,
Let them flow in ceaseless praise.'

It's about time many of us discovered her kind of commitment for ourselves. We should stop saying to the Lord, 'I'm tired', 'I'm busy' or 'I'm booked up' . . . or a thousand similar excuses. It's about time we started paying the cost of discipleship.

St. Paul summed it all up when he wrote;

'So then, my brothers, because of God's great mercy to us I appeal to you: Offer yourselves as a living sacrifice to God, dedicated to His service and pleasing to Him.'

The right time

Jesus always seemed to be in the right place at the right time. He was constantly open to His Father's will. When He reached Sychar, en route from Judaea to Galilee, He was really tired. It had been a hot and dusty journey.

As He sat by Jacob's well in the mid-day heat He must have felt ready for a rest. He could have easily ignored the Samaritan woman who went there to draw water. Anyway, it was unheard of for a Jewish religious leader to mix with Samaritans . . . let alone a Samaritan woman.

But as she came to the well Jesus was available to her. He saw her guilt, her failure and her spiritual thirst. There and then the woman responded to His call and went back to town to tell everyone that she had met the Messiah.

We don't draw water from wells, but we do meet people in equally mundane situations. Places like the supermarket, the garage forecourt, or in the street. When we begin to say 'anytime' to the Lord we become available, even in the daily routine, to be in the right place at the right time.

Chance meetings, and friendly conversations take on a whole new meaning when you've said 'anytime' to the Lord. You begin to look for God incidents, rather than coincidences.

A friend of mine was travelling by rail to Birmingham. He was going to visit his girlfriend for the weekend. He'd had a difficult week at medical school, and he was tired. He sat opposite a woman who was looking rather bored. They began to talk. It was the usual list of subjects. The weather, bad rail journeys, chat about family and friends.

My friend shared his faith in a natural and spontaneous way, and the woman seemed interested. She asked him a lot of questions about Christianity, so my friend took out his Bible and read several verses to her. She seemed close to making a commitment to Christ.

The train reached Birmingham, but before my friend left he gave the woman his Bible and wrote his name and address in the front cover. She promised to write to him. As my friend got off, a Christian girl got on the train. She was travelling to the West Country. As she walked up the aisle she noticed the woman reading the Bible. There was an empty seat beside her. The Christian girl was able to carry on the conversation where my friend had ended. Before the end of the journey that passenger had given her life to Christ, and she wrote to my friend to tell him.

Coincidence? I don't think so. Here were two Christians who were open to the Lord's guidance 'anytime'. Because of that commitment, they found themselves in the right train seat at the right time.

God is the Potter, we are the clay. Until we offer Him all of our time we remain unworkable lumps in His hands. Until we say 'anytime' we aren't much use in His Kingdom.

6: *Anyone*

Someone decided that our church needed some new crockery. I don't know why because we had more than enough already! A local pottery gave us a huge quantity absolutely free of charge. It seemed like a real bargain. The tea chest full of cups, saucers and plates arrived at my door 'for the church'.

There had to be a catch in it somewhere . . . and there was! It was all useless. The saucers wobbled, the plates were out of shape, and the cups didn't have handles. It was just rubbish. It was not fit for use or ornament and was soon despatched to the rubbish tip.

Unless our lives are firmly in the Potter's grip and shaped by Him we'll end up much the same. Our lives will be spoiled by selfishness, prejudice and bitterness. We'll be of no use in His Kingdom. Jesus Christ needs to mould and shape our attitudes towards other people. He needs to break down our prejudices, wipe out any bitterness, and give us resources of compassion to care for people.

I have identified five different groups of people which have sometimes tested my patience! Only through the grace and love of Jesus have I been able to go on loving them. Maybe you'll be able to identify other groups that give you problems.

Irritating People

I fumbled for the keys to the minibus. It was dark and the rain was pouring down. The gang of teenage lads was getting restless. I opened the rear door and let them in. They had been quite well behaved during the youth meeting, but now they were in high spirits. It was time to head for home. We drove away from the Hackney church into the stream of London traffic.

The journey back to Deptford wasn't an easy one. My gang of passengers seemed determined to make it memorable! They rocked the minibus from side to side, made rude faces out of the rear window, and sang bawdy songs at the top of their voices.

I soon reached the limits of my patience, so I pulled into the verge and gave them a stern warning. They could either shut up . . . or start walking! On we went through the Rotherhithe tunnel and along the dark South London streets.

As we drew up outside the church in Deptford I sighed with relief. Just as I was letting my passengers out the tubby caretaker of the church burst through the church doors.

'You lot are in big trouble, you've really done it now!', he muttered. 'If you're not all back in Hackney in thirty minutes you'll have to face the police.'

The gang let out a loud groan of disapproval. I turned the vehicle round and headed back towards Hackney. An air of gloom descended on the group, and they all fell silent.

The Hackney minister greeted us at the door of the church. 'Look lads,' he explained, 'there's a wallet gone missing and an old man is very upset, because it contained his money and his pension book. Okay lads, a joke's a joke — let's have it back, and the matter need go no further.'

There was an uneasy silence. The gang looked at each other as they tried to work out whether to speak or keep silent. This uneasy silence continued for several minutes, then one of the lads said, 'It's in the gent's toilet — third cistern along. We didn't mean any harm.'

The Hackney minister went off to look and returned a few minutes later with the wallet held high. The lads apologised, if rather half-heartedly, and the minister beamed at us.

As the lads boarded the minibus I went back and apologized to the minister. I felt responsible. I was really fed up, and I felt like closing the youth club down. It all seemed such a pointless waste of time.

Walter, the Hackney minister, took one look at me and roared with laughter! 'Why on earth are you looking like that? This is nothing! You should see some of the scrapes I've landed myself in. I've spent most of my ministry chasing naughty kids around church premises . . . but that's what it's all about. The minute we stop caring for kids like these we might as well give up!'

I knew that he was right. Over the years I've remembered his advice when I've been in worse scrapes. It isn't easy to care for kids who vandalise church premises, who prefer rock music to conversation, and who disappear whenever you need their help!

Yet Jesus calls us to care for irritating people. It really saddens me when I hear of youth leaders or of churches who have 'given up on the young people'. They have turned their backs on a great opportunity. Only recently I heard that a youth club was closed down because a mirror had been broken. The church council ruled that these youngsters were no longer welcome on church premises because they 'broke too much', didn't pay enough, and were too badly behaved.

In saying you will serve 'anyone' for the Lord, you must include the people that drive you mad. They may be very elderly or very young or anywhere in between . . . but the irritating people of this world need to know the love of Christ. If we don't take time out to care for them . . . who will?

Incompatible people

If we are realistic, all of us know people whom we find it hard to get on with. They may not have the same interests as us, or they may just see things very differently. Whatever the reason, we find it hard work to talk to them.

Sometimes when we open the front door and see someone like this it's very hard to seem pleased to see them. The temptation is to make some excuse and get rid of them as quickly as we can!

Dr. William Sangster, one of Methodism's most famous preachers, knew how hard it was to care for people like this. When he was a minister at Aintree near Liverpool he was very busy. He had been overworking, and he was feeling tired. He used to write some personal notes to pinpoint areas of personal failure as a Christian. In one of them he wrote, 'I am deceitful in that I often express private annoyance when a caller is announced and simulate pleasure when I actually greet them!'

I know exactly what he meant! I realise in my own life that surface smiles and polite welcomes are not genuine love. It's not enough for us to be pleasant to people . . . we should learn how to love them.

The Lord often seems to put us in situations with people whom we wouldn't normally choose as friends. But often I have discovered that if I work at a relationship I can be pleasantly surprised!

My wife Jacqui was put in a situation just like this. Before she went to Kenya to work with the Church Missionary Society, she had to go on a preparation course. She knew that at the end of the course she would be partnered with another girl from the group. They would be stationed together for a year in the African bush. As Jacqui looked around the room at the other Christian girls she wondered with whom she would be partnered. As she looked around she prayed, 'Lord, let it be anyone except Jo.'

But the Lord had different plans, and she was asked to team up with Jo! They lived together in a tiny cottage, cooked over wood fires and taught in a Kenyan girls' school. They faced many different crises, adventures and hilarious moments. Over that year they discovered a real respect for each other and became close friends. When Jacqui and I got married, Jo was our bridesmaid. Jacqui and Jo had grown as close as sisters.

When we offer to serve 'anyone', the Lord will lead us to new friends and into richer relationships than we could ever have imagined. Through the grace and love of Jesus Christ we can make people we find 'incompatible' our closest friends!

I'm sure that the Lord brings people into our lives for a purpose; if we turn our backs on them we are missing the plan and purpose that He has for us. We are not really available for Him to use for 'anyone'.

Infuriating People

Some people really make us mad! They may have wronged us, hurt us or rejected us. Whenever we see them we feel ourselves tensing up, and our minds filling up with all kinds of uncharitable thoughts!

It's not easy to go on loving those who push us away — or whose actions have caused us immeasurable hurt and pain. Yet they form part of the circle of people with whom we must mix. They are people we must go on serving and loving.

One of my friends is a minister in a Lancashire town, and there are some people who have really criticised his ministry. He has developed a wonderful technique for serving people who hurt him . . . he bakes them a cake! When I asked him why he did this he explained, 'It's my way of loving them to bits!' I admired his courage. To meet criticism with compassion demands a really Christian spirit.

Jesus taught us that we should love our enemies and pray for the people who persecute us. He said,

'Why should God reward you if you love only the people who love you? Even the tax-gatherers do that! And if you speak only to your friends, have you done anything out of the ordinary? Even the pagans do that!'

It can be costly to say 'anyone you send, Lord, I will love.' For He may just ask us to serve those who have hurt us deeply, and even scarred our lives. This is the quality of grace which enabled Jesus to declare from the cross,

'Father, forgive them.'

Ananias was a man who was willing to reach out and forgive, no matter what the cost. He lived in Damascus and was a committed Christian and a good witness for the Lord. One day he heard that Saul of Tarsus was on his way into town. This proud Jew was arriving to break up the church and to put all the Christians into jail. It must have been a terrifying time for all the Christians in Damascus.

Just then Ananias felt the Lord calling him to go and witness to Saul. It was asking rather a lot! After all, such a meeting could cost him his life! It would have probably seemed wise to go into hiding until Saul left town.

But Ananias obeyed the Lord's call and went to the house of Judas in Straight Street where Saul was staying. He knew that Saul, the enemy of the Church, was there — his knees must have been knocking as he went in. Yet the first words that Ananias spoke were, 'Brother Saul'. He was willing to leave behind his anger and fear and reach out to the person who threatened him most. It must have taken guts!

Saul had seen a blinding light while travelling towards Damascus, and he'd heard the voice of Christ. He was wandering blind and confused in that no-man's-land between conviction and conversion. He was in a terrible state.

Ananias was able to care for him and witness to him. Saul became a Chirstian and was baptised. He was re-named Paul, and went on to become the greatest missionary the church has ever known. All because Ananias cared for his enemy!

What greater modern example of this kind of loving could there be than Corrie Ten Boom? That little Dutch lady with the big heart and the kind of faith that stood the test of suffering.

Years after her ordeal in the Ravensbruck concentration camp she met one of the German officers who had cruelly mistreated her. It took all her trust in Jesus to look him in the face and shake him by the hand.

As she reached out to the 'enemy' she felt the power of the Holy Spirit flowing through her. She was able to do what she thought would be impossible. I'm sure that when we move to forgive those who have wronged us the Spirit moves with us.

Through the power of the Holy Spirit we can achieve the impossible.

Inferior People

Few of us would ever admit that we feel superior to others. Yet if the truth were known, many of us demonstrate this kind of snobbishness in our daily lives.

I have shared in courses on 'racism awareness' and seen how people who refuse to admit they are racist are finally made aware of their prejudice. Our prejudices against others are sometimes only camouflaged by a veneer of politeness.

Jesus had a knack of seeing right through prejudice. He disliked it intensely. He mixed with the outcasts of His generation, and seemed to care most for people who society rejected. He cast the Samaritan, the second class citizen of His time, in the hero's role in His parable of the Good Samaritan.

Sadly, we sometimes see the prejudices of the world displayed in the Church. This was made clear to me when I took a friend of mine to sing at a large suburban church near Blackpool.

Big John was an ex-car thief from Manchester. The first time I met him I wondered what I'd let myself in for. He came to work with me on a mission and the moment he arrived I nearly sent him straight back! He clambered out of an old Land Rover with hair down to his shoulders and a long drooping moustache. His Mohican-style jacket, earring, and battered guitar all added to his unorthodox image.

I quickly discovered that John was a fine Christian with a great testimony. He wrote some beautiful gospel songs, and sang with a joy and conviction that really made people listen.

When we arrived at the church near Blackpool he realised that it wasn't his scene, but he was willing to give it a try. We were both quite nervous as we strolled down the church aisle towards the vestry. It was going to be a big youth service.

We greeted a few of the older church members as we walked through the church. Just then, I overheard one deaf lady whispering loudly to another, 'We don't like his type here' as she pointed to my friend John.

They were guilty of the same prejudice against John as me. To them John was some kind of drop-out. A no-good. Someone to be avoided. They didn't want to associate with him. It was a real indictment of their shallow form of Christianity. They were blinded by prejudice.

The incident reminded me of that old preacher's yarn about the black man who tried to go to an all-white church in a Southern State in America. He was forcefully ejected and told not to come back. Sitting outside the church as the service continued he felt miserable and rejected. The Lord appeared to him and comforted him by saying 'Don't worry, they won't let me in either!'

When we say 'anyone' to the Lord we had better realise what this means. For the 'anyone' that He sends may reveal whole areas of prejudice deep within us which we hardly knew existed. The 'anyone' may be an Asian, or a West Indian, a selfish millionaire with a big cigar. It could be a drop-out, or a fat lady with a mink coat. Or what if it were a criminal, an addict, or someone with an old school tie?

Wherever our prejudices lie — whether we be a snob or an 'inverted snob' — we are sure to be in for a big surprise! The Lord has a habit of sending just the kind of person we'd really rather not see!

St. Paul wrote to the Corinthians:

'I am a free man, nobody's slave; but I make myself everybody's slave in order to win as many people as possible. While working with the Jews, I live like a Jew in order to win them; and even though I myself am not subject to the Law of Moses, I live as though I were when working with those who are, in order to win them. In the same way, when working with Gentiles, I live like a Gentile, outside the Jewish Law, in order to win Gentiles.'

This statement was not an easy one for Paul to make. He was a Jew born of the tribe of Benjamin. He had been trained in the Law by Gamaliel. What was more he was a Pharisee, one of the Jewish elite. He had everything going for him in the Jewish society from which he came. It was unthinkable for someone from such a social background to mix with people of other races, let alone to love them! Yet Paul was willing to count his privileged background as nothing for the sake of serving Christ.

Paul had to ditch his feelings of superiority and start getting alongside people!

When we have identified our deep rooted prejudices, we need to let Jesus Christ deal with them. As the Lord changes us we will begin to see people as He sees them. It will not matter what their colour, creed or social background is . . . they will simply be people to love and to serve in Christ's name.

Individual People

I'm sure that sometimes the Lord brings even those who seem totally self-sufficient and in control of their lives to us so that we can serve them and care for them. Even they have moments of desperate need.

It's so easy to be totally pre-occupied with our own lives and to fail to see that people around us are in such need. We call 'How are you?', but don't wait for a reply. We offer help, but don't really expect people to take us up on it.

The 'servant' lifestyle doesn't seem very popular today. We would all rather 'be served' than serve others. Yet we follow a Saviour who washed His disciples' feet and who declared,

> 'You call me teacher and Lord, and it is right that you do so, because that is what I am. I, your Lord and Teacher, have just washed your feet. You, then, should wash one another's feet. I have set an example for you.'

This ministry of service is one of the most costly aspects of Christian discipleship . . . yet it's one of the most rewarding. We're not only called to serve other Christians, we're called to serve all who are in need. The Bible teaches that this quality of service is the hallmark of our faith. James wrote:

'But someone will say, "One person has faith, another has actions." My answer is, "Show me how anyone can have faith without actions. I will show you my faith by my actions."'

Jesus comes to us in the needs of individuals all around us. Yet we're so caught up with ourselves and our own interests that we hardly notice. In one of His most powerful statements on judgement, Jesus made it clear that some of us would have to pay dearly for our uncaring attitudes.

In His parable of the sheep and the goats some people were sure that they had never seen the King hungry, thirsty, lonely, naked, sick or in prison. If they had ever seen the King in need they would have raced to help him! But the King retorted,

'I tell you, whenever you refused to help one of these least important ones, you refused to help me.'

When we say 'anyone' to the Lord, we are offering to serve 'anyone in need'. For in serving 'anyone in need' we are in fact serving Jesus Christ. For He comes to us in the suffering of the individuals who surround us. Behind the net curtains of every street there are broken, hurting people. In every circle of friends there are those whose smiling faces may hide their need of our help. In every family there are people with special needs. What a transformation there would be if we all stopped using others, and started letting them use us! We would really be living out Christ's commission to love one another.

Two teenage girls from our youth fellowship took this to heart when they 'adopted a granny'. The very elderly lady they 'adopted' never had a visitor. She was desperately lonely.

The two girls began to visit her every week. They took gifts to her, they cut her lawn, and walked her to the end of her garden and back. Their visits were never mentioned in the press or heralded as important by the local community. Yet for that one lonely old lady their visits were priceless. It meant for her the re-birth of hope. Someone cared at last.

When we give our lives to the Potter, we must be willing to love 'anyone' He sends our way. Once we grasp this, we will begin to see people in a completely new way. We will stop judging people, and start loving them. Before long, our circle of friends will grow wider and wider. And our lives will be all the richer.

7: Anything

When I was on a mission in Northern Ireland I went to visit a Christian friend whom I hadn't seen for ten years. I went to meet him in an old garden where he spent time in prayer every day. I opened the garden gate and stepped inside. It creaked shut behind me. The ornamental garden was overgrown. Weeds covered the flowerbeds, and the fountains were silent. There was an air of past splendour about the place.

My friend was sitting on a rickety bench in the middle of the garden. He was praying, but he turned to greet me as he heard me approach. It was great to see him again. We had so much news to share since we'd last met. We talked about our friends and families. Somehow, he seemed different. He appeared so much gentler than I remembered him. His old arrogance had gone. I remembered him as a staunch Protestant with a bitter hatred of Catholics. But that had gone too. There was now something very gracious about him.

After a while he explained what had happened. He had realised that his commitment to Christ was incomplete. He was willing to do anything but love Catholics. God convicted him of his bitterness and broke down his hatred. God then called him to work with the priests and nuns in one of Belfast's toughest downtown areas. In painful obedience he went, and discovered the presence of Christ among his new colleagues. Gradually his deep-rooted prejudice was removed and he was free to love.

The one thing that he was unwilling to do was the very thing God wanted! He could not find the deepening relationship with Jesus Christ that he wanted until he was willing to give in completely to God.

The Lord has a strange way of highlighting those areas of our lives which we're holding back; and of asking us to do the very things we're unwilling to do! Until we're willing to do 'anything' we're not really available for the Lord to use!

This kind of commitment is very demanding. It is the kind of commitment which sent Livingstone to Africa, Whitfield to America, Aylward to China . . . or Wesley riding through every part of England. They were willing to do 'anything' that the Lord asked, no matter what it involved. They were willing to pay the price.

How cheap and how mean much of our commitment to Christ really is. Many of us would be more truthful if we said we'd do 'nothing' for the Lord. Very few Christians seem willing to do 'anything'. Many Christians today can barely spare an hour a week for worship, let alone a life-time for service. We tend to give the Lord the left-overs.

Jesus made it clear that commitment to Him was not easy. Following Him may involve us laying down our lives. Jesus said,

> 'Whoever comes to me cannot be my disciple unless he loves me more than he loves his father and his mother, his wife and his children, his brothers and his sisters, and himself as well. Whoever does not carry his own cross and come after me cannot be my disciple.'

William Stringfellow summed it up when he wrote,

> 'A Christian looks like a sucker because he is free to give his own life. To die imminently for the sake of anyone or anything at all. Even those or that which seems unworthy of his death, thereby cele-

69

brating the one who died for all, though none be
worthy . . . not even one.'

Our commitment to do 'anything' for the Lord is something we should constantly be renewing. What God is
asking of us in our teenage years may be very different
to what He expects when we're in our sixties. John
Wesley realised how important this ongoing renewal of
our commitment is. In August 1755 he used a simple
order of service called the 'Covenant Service'. It was a
powerful occasion of re-dedication, and he used it regu-
larly afterwards. Methodists all over the world still hold
annual 'Covenant Services'. They still use the basic
outline prepared by John Wesley. Sometimes the service
is held in September, when the new Methodist church
year begins, but most often it is held on the first Sunday
in January.

Whenever it is held, it is a deeply challenging act of
worship. The covenant promise, which is at the heart of
the service, really takes the 'ifs and buts' out of Christian
commitment. It cuts through the apathy of much of our
modern commitment and asks big things of us. It reads:

> 'I am no longer my own, but yours. Put me to what
> you will, rank me with whom you will; put me to
> doing, put me to suffering; let me be employed for
> you or laid aside for you, exalted for you or brought
> low for you; let me be full, let me be empty; let me
> have all things, let me have nothing; I freely and
> wholeheartedly yield all things to your pleasure and
> disposal.'

I find this promise harder to make as the years go by.
It's not that my commitment to Christ is weakening, but
that the truth of what it may involve grows more real to
me. For as we say 'anything' to Him, he often takes us

up on our commitment. Let's look at the covenant promise in detail, and really search our hearts.

'I am no longer my own, but yours'

It's so easy to lull ourselves into thinking that we are doing rather a lot for the Lord. This phrase is a haunting reminder of what Christian commitment really involves. Only as we resign our lives completely into His hands will we discover how He wishes to use us.

During the Boxer Revolution in China, a young minister was arrested. The Red Guard took him for interrogation. After some time the authorities prepared the papers for his release. There was only one condition . . . he had to sign a declaration denying his faith. Naturally, he refused. Day after day and week after week the guards returned with the document. If only he would sign he could go free. It was a very distressing experience — for he was cut off from his family and friends. Ten years went by. The pressure grew intolerable. Finally, he signed the papers. He renounced his faith in Christ and was allowed to go back home. Within six months, however, he went back to the authorities and destroyed the document. He was promptly thrown back in jail. He was imprisoned there for many more years.

Dr. Edwin Orr, the much travelled preacher, met this minister recently. He asked him what made him return to the authorities and destroy the document he had signed. He answered, 'I'd rather live without freedom than live without Jesus.'

When our lives truly belong to Jesus Christ we will genuinely want what He wants. Our lives will not be something which we grasp and cling hold of . . . but something which we give and share.

St Paul declared, 'For me to live is Christ, to die is gain'. It didn't matter to him whether he lived or whether he died, his life was totally given over to Jesus. He was no longer his own, but the Lord's.

There is a great freedom in giving our lives over to Jesus. Suddenly, we are available to be used in all kinds of situations we would previously have considered 'beyond us'!

'Put me to what you will, rank me with whom you will.'

Wesley's covenant promise doesn't say, 'Put me to what I'm capable of'. It says, 'Put me to what you will'. I'm sure that the Lord sometimes calls us into areas of service for which we feel utterly incapable. Sometimes the jobs he gives seem bigger than our natural gifts and abilities to deal with them.

The Old Testament prophet Jeremiah didn't really feel capable of what God was asking of him. When he heard that God wanted him to be a prophet to the nations he replied,

'Sovereign Lord, I don't know how to speak, I am too young.'

But the Lord made short work of Jeremiah's excuses, and told him to forget his youth and go! History proved that Jeremiah was the man for the job; and even though he felt incapable he was used in a wonderful way.

Even now, after ten active years in the ministry, I still find myself approaching situations that I don't know how to handle. Sometimes I have stood outside the home of a bereaved family not knowing what to say. Or I have stood in church vestries feeling unworthy to go and preach the Word. But I have found again and again in my own life that where God calls — He equips.

Commissioner Catherine Bramwell Booth of the Salvation Army has found this to be true in her experience. She once said,

'It's a very strange experience living so closely to death as I do now — I don't want to die, and I'm in love with life. Now I look back I feel, 'O wasn't it wonderful — and how God helped me when my best wasn't good enough.'

This section of the covenant continues with the words 'Rank me with whom you will.' When I say it, I'm reminded of the times when I've worked alongside Naval Chaplains. They have no rank in the Navy. Because of this, they can mix freely with seamen and admirals. They can get alongside anyone.

In serving Christ we must be willing to work with anyone — and to do anything. This kind of dedication brings a great freedom into our discipleship. We will find our lives full of wonderful surprises! And as we follow His call He will equip us and go with us.

'Put me to doing, put me to suffering'

One dark January night as I was saying farewell to the departing congregation after a Covenant Service an angry old man came up to me. 'That bit about suffering is ridiculous,' he said, 'I don't want any suffering. I refused to say it!'

I tried to explain that should suffering be part of our experience, we should be willing to go through it for the Lord. Whatever God's plan for our lives should involve, we should be ready to accept it and use it for His glory.

If our faith collapses when we face suffering, it can't be very real. If we are not willing to suffer for God's glory it will surely make us bitter and broken people. We must be willing for the Lord to ask us to do anything . . . even to suffer.

I only wish the old man could have been with me the day a reporter from a London radio station came to see me. He had come to visit members of the congregation and to interview them on the meaning of Good Friday. The completed programme was to be broadcast during prime time that Good Friday morning.

We drove a couple of miles from the church to a small

terraced house in the South London side street. Jessie welcomed us into her home and made us tea. We sat and talked for some time, and then the reporter started setting up his tape recorder.

Jessie spoke of the way that she had recently learned that she had terminal cancer. She had only a few more months to live. She was trying to come to terms with the short time she had left, and to discover how best to use it. With a glowing smile she spoke of her love for Jesus Christ, and of the way that He knew what it was to suffer. For He had died on a cross. She was convinced that whatever lay ahead Jesus would go with her, and that His strength would support her.

The reporter was moved by what he'd heard. He quietly packed up the recorder and left. But the quiet assurance which Jessie conveyed wasn't just something she put on for the interview. She was quite prepared to use her suffering for God's glory, and God's peace filled her life completely.

I watched her over those last months. What she said on the radio programme was for real. She eventually lay on her hospital bed for weeks, unable to move or even to speak. But there was a peace and radiance that shone from her that impressed the whole ward. She suffered for the glory of God. And that's perhaps the most powerful witness of all.

'Let me be employed for you or laid aside for you'

Activists like myself find these words some of the hardest to say. Many people who enjoy a hectic lifestyle and ever-changing opportunities for service dread the thought of stopping. Of reaching a time when the work is over and all the tasks complete.

The Methodist preacher previously mentioned, Dr. William Sangster, was a real activist. He darted about the country leading missions and preaching with power and vision. Right at the height of his ministry when he had so much to do he learnt that he had muscular atrophy.

It was a devastating blow. His movements were laboured, and he felt constantly tired. Eventually he found it hard to speak. His preaching, which thousands gathered to hear, grew more and more difficult. One humiliating day he fell down in the street and was too weak to get up.

In his letter of resignation to his church he wrote, 'God has never been nearer to me than now. I have had grace never to murmur. Infinite wisdom and infinite love are at work for me — and a man who is sure of that can endure anything.'

Sangster was genuinely willing to be employed for the Lord, or laid aside for Him. Many of us are unwilling to take the same kind of step. It can be very difficult to leave behind certain jobs when the Lord calls us to new duties. Sometimes I've met people who hold on to jobs or responsibilities they should leave behind. They are unwilling to admit to themselves, or to others, that they are indispensable. They risk blocking God's will for their own lives, and for the people they serve.

Part of saying 'anything' to the Lord is a willingness to be laid aside. It's a realisation that, after all it is God's work and not ours. It takes a lot of humility to step down, and to encourage those who take our place.

'Exalted for you or brought low for you'

Once I came across a sign in a village church vestry which read, 'You can't convince people that you're a good preacher and that Christ is a wonderful Saviour.' It has challenged me ever since.

Whatever form of service he may call us to undertake, we must do it for His glory and not our own. For no matter how gifted we may be our work will not bring honour to Christ if we are keeping some of the praise for ourselves. Once we are genuinely serving Christ and glorifying His Name it doesn't really matter whether we are are exalted, or brought low. The only thing that matters is that Jesus is glorified.

Over the years I have discovered that often when we choose the path of humility our work is all the more effective. Very often the things which have given me the greatest joy in my ministry are the things which have gone unnoticed by everyone else.

It is difficult to keep walking the path of humility; and we all get a bit big-headed from time to time. In saying 'Let me be exalted for you, or brought low for you' we are giving Christ the glory in advance, and accepting with joy whatever comes our way.

'Let me be full, let me be empty; Let me have all things, let me have nothing'

I drove the huge automatic car from Kennedy airport through the Manhattan traffic toward the centre of town. It was a real strain. I was tired after the long trans-Atlantic flight, and the sweltering heat was exhausting.

As my wife navigated with a small road map we made our way to one of the poorer inner-city areas of New York. The young minister welcomed us with a kind of caring attitude that made us feel at home straight away. We were to treat his home as our own. We were part of the family.

We discovered that we were in a Filipino ghetto area near the heart of New York City. In the church meetings that weekend we heard something of the terrible problems which faced the people there.

The young minister had left the affluence of suburbia in order to work with the people here. He could have earned much higher salary in one of the smarter areas of the State, but he was willing to bear the cost of working just where God wanted him to work. It had really cut his standard of living.

A few days later we drove the huge hire car through

the beautiful woodland of New England to stay with another minister in Vermont. His situation was very different. His congregation was affluent and prosperous and they could afford to pay their minister well. His two large homes, three cars, speedboat and high standard of living were beyond anything I'd experienced in England.

Yet he displayed a spirit of generosity which was quite wonderful. He paid all the living expenses of our mission team while we were in the States, and shared everything he had with us. As we water-skied across the lake near his country home he praised the Lord for the things that he had; and the opportunity to share them with us. He knew that he was only holding those possessions in trust, and he wanted to use them for others as fully as he could.

Whether we own a lot or very little we must realise that we are only holding these things 'in trust'. We must share what we have completely and give to those in need with joy and generosity. If we really live by this principle it won't be our aim in life to own more . . . but to share more. It will enable us to let the Lord set our standard of living rather than the cost of living index, or the Joneses next door.

'I freely and wholeheartedly yield all things to your pleasure and disposal'

God is the Potter, and we are the clay. He must use us in the ways in which He thinks best. Paul wrote:

> 'But who are you, my friend, to answer God back? A clay pot does not ask the man who made it, "Why did you make me like this?" After all, the man who makes the pots has the right to use the clay as he wishes, and to make two pots from the same lump of clay, one for special occasions and the other for ordinary use.'

As we offer Him 'all things to His pleasure and disposal' it won't matter so much what He is calling us to do. It could mean international acclaim or total obscurity; it could mean a major television series or a job in the Sunday school creche. What will matter is that we're walking in His will.

Too many Christians are desperate to fulfil their own ambitions. They are pre-occupied with earthly rewards and aren't really seeking to do the Lord's will. Too many of us are avoiding areas of work and service because we feel 'it's not our sort of thing'. We don't feel worthy enough or gifted enough, and we're not willing to launch out in faith. And there are lots of us who see serving Christ in terms of a scale of status. We recognise some jobs as 'important' and others as 'menial', so we avoid the humbler tasks. Yet God sees all forms of service as equally valuable and important.

God's plan and purpose for our lives is the perfect one. As we offer to do 'anything' for Him we really become like clay in His hands. And as He moulds us and shapes us He will reveal possibilities that are beyond our wildest dreams . . .

8: Everything

I had been in Kenya for several weeks on a project called 'Share our Faith'. I was rapidly discovering that I had a lot more to learn than to share. Day after day I met people whose commitment to Jesus Christ made me feel ashamed. The Kenyan Christians seemed to have a joy and radiance that made our British Christianity seem dull.

One day we went on a long and dusty drive. We arrived at the village feeling hungry and thirsty. I didn't feel very overjoyed by the thought of a procession and service in that heat.

Eventually the procession got under way, and we slowly marched through the mud hut village and out into the fields beyond. The crowd was in a joyful mood, and they sang beautiful African hymns in harmony. The tall green sugar cane swayed in the warm breeze, and the heat rose from the road in a shimmering haze. We walked for over half an hour, and I wondered where we were going.

I felt rather uneasy about my own lack of enthusiasm for the event. After all, some of the people had walked for several days through the bush to be a part of the celebration. I heard how some of them had slept rough, and made their way from distant villages to be with us that day. They didn't seem tired, however, and the singing certainly didn't drag!

As we continued, I began to get caught up in the spirit of the event. Their joy and enthusiasm blessed me. I began to sense the presence of God with us in that slow procession. The leaders of the procession halted, and then turned into a rough field covered with tall dry grass. The people followed them across the field towards four overgrown mounds.

The singing stopped, and an air of reverence silenced the crowd. One of the ministers leading the procession took me by the arm to the four mounds, and the people crowded round. Some whispered quietly to each other, but others stood with fixed expressions. The crickets continued their ceaseless chatter, but there was still an intensity of silence there. A very old lady, who was almost bent double with age, began to sing an old gospel hymn in Swahili. Her dry wrinkled face was alive with the joy of her faith. Soon the whole crowd was singing too.

The minister beside me explained that the four mounds were the graves of British missionaries. They had been murdered by the villagers many years before. The missionaries had not died in vain. For through their death the village had received the gospel, and this was an area where thousands of people had become Christians. I looked down at the four graves. There were no names or inscriptions. And in the quietness, I thanked God for these unknown missionaries and their willingness to die for their faith.

My seven week visit to Kenya was quickly over, but it made an indelible impression on my life. The people I met there seemed to take the meaning of discipleship seriously, and I came home deeply convicted of my own half-heartedness. The texts which I had read so often in the past seemed to take on new life and meaning for me. I began to realise that to live for Christ meant that I should let my 'old self' completely die for him. I don't think that I had really experienced what that meant in daily living before then. Texts like Galatians 2.20 suddenly burst into life for me:

'I have been put to death with Christ on his cross,

80

> so that it is no longer I who live, but it is Christ
> who lives in me. This life that I live now, I live by
> faith in the Son of God, who loves me and gives his
> life for me.'

The starting point for all Christian living must be the
death of our old selves. The clay must be willing to lose
its old shape if it is to discover its new form.

The potter takes it and squeezes it, and presses it and
kneads it . . . and places it on the wheel. And as the
wheel spins he gives it a new shape and a new purpose.
From the breaking of the old form comes the birth of
the new.

Let's look at the words of Galatians closely with appli-
cation to each of our own lives.

'I have been put to death with Christ on his cross'

Three of my friends were climbing in North Wales one
wintry day when a terrible electric storm began. They
were surrounded by brilliant streaks of lightning, so they
took cover as best they could. Lower down the mountain
someone was struck by lightning and terribly injured;
and as my friends sheltered from the storm they were
very aware that their lives were in danger.

One of the three looked up into the sky and saw a
great streak of lightning shooting through the air towards
him. He knew in that instant that he would be hit.

In that fraction of time as the lightning shot towards
him the climber saw a vision. It was as if time stood
still, and he saw his life before him in a solid block. He
saw every decision, every turning point and every
mistake he had made.

Though he was struck by the lightning, he miracu-
lously escaped; but more important to him than its
physical impact was the spiritual impact on his life of
what he had seen.

I wonder what we would see if we were to glimpse

that vision of our past? How many bad decisions, wrong thoughts and evil motives would we see paraded before us? I wonder if our lives would appear as one great heap of self-centredness? Would a glimpse through our past fill us with regret?

Maybe all of us need to recognise that our old lives have not been put to death with Christ on the cross. We have meddled around with Christianity, but not known the real thing. We have not truly given Him our past, all that we are and all that we hope to become.

If we are to be clay in the Potter's hand we must die to self. If we are to become what He intends we must lose our old form and let Him shape the new.

'So that it is no longer I who live'

A young man who worked in a large engineering factory in Lancashire had committed himself to Christ, and was sincerely wanting the Lord to rule and control his life.

One coffee break, at work, he took a piece of paper and a biro and scribbled down some words. Though he hadn't written any poems or songs before, the words he wrote seemed to flow perfectly. That evening, he managed to put some music to the words, and he began to sing the song as part of his witness to young people in the youth club that he ran.

It was a very simple song, and he had no idea what would happen to it. Over the years that song has been sung in thousands of churches and youth meetings all over the world. It has been translated into many languages and incorporated into many hymn books.

Yet, for Keith White, that song was just a simple expression of what the Lord was doing in his life. He wrote:

'For me to live is Christ, to die is gain,
To hold His hand, and walk his narrow way,
There is no peace, no joy, no thrill,

Like walking in His will,
For me to live, is Christ, to die is gain.

Keith had discovered that his life needed to be totally Christ-centred. It it wasn't, his witness would be ineffective and his lifestyle unattractively self-centred.

Each of us needs to put Jesus Christ at the very centre and focus of all that we are. The starting point for true discipleship must be the death of self and the Lordship of Jesus Christ over our every action. It's so easy to go running for Jesus, only to discover that He's not running with us! To go witnessing for Him, but give ourselves all the glory. To go out serving others, only to realise that our own resources don't keep us going very long.

Our lives need to be filled and flooded with His Power and His presence. He needs to be at the centre of everything. He needs to take control of every part of our personality. He needs to live within us — 'so that it is no longer I who live'.

'But it is Christ who lives in me'

I opened the back door and called in. 'Do come in,' the old lady called back. I went into the dark little kitchen and on into the dingy lounge. The lady was hunched over the flickering gas fire — she welcomed me and invited me to sit down beside her.

The walls were lined with old brown photographs. One showed a soldier dressed for the Great War. There was a family photo with a group of ladies in bonnets. There were pictures of an old country chapel, and an open air meeting. There was a pile of unopened tinned food on the table, and a few Christmas cards in a pile on the shelf. It was hard to believe that it was Christmas Day. She'd had nothing to eat.

This was the first of many visits to this ninety-five year old Christian. Though she had been housebound for many years, and rarely had a visitor, she was radiantly happy. Every time I visited her she would dig out more old photgraphs, and she would share different adventures from her life. As she looked back over her life she rejoiced at all the wonderful ways in which the Lord had blessed and guided her. She had a quality of peace and love which I have rarely seen in anyone else. Here was a person whose life was, to say the least, rather monotonous. She sat in that little room year in and year out, but she really knew that Christ lived within her. When she prayed with me, or sang some old gospel song to me, I became deeply aware of the presence of Christ in that depressing old room. She was cut off from fellowship, and she was deprived of much that makes life exciting — but she wasn't cut off from Jesus.

Like any relationship, we must spend time developing and strengthening our friendship with Jesus Christ. For He must never be someone who lives on the perimeter of our being, but someone who 'lives in me'.

'This life that I live now, I live by faith in the Son of God'

One night I was preaching at a huge suburban church. The hymn before the sermon drew to an end and I climbed up the pulpit steps. There were several hundred people in the congregation, and I was feeling rather nervous. As I launched into my sermon the door at the far end of the church swung open and a middle aged man entered and sat in the back pew. It is strange how individuals can sometimes become noticeable among a large congregation, and I was especially aware of him throughout the service.

At the end of the sermon I invited people to come forward and make a fresh commitment to Jesus Christ. As the last hymn began the man who had arrived late made his way to the front.

He was broken that night, and knelt humbly before the large central cross. Some time later he wrote to me to explain what had happened. That night he had been returning from a preaching appointment, and had seen the lights on in the church. He had been curious to see what the service was like, so he had joined us just in time for the sermon. That evening he became aware that, even though he was a preacher, he had 'lost his grip on Jesus'.

I'm sure that many of us are attempting to serve the Lord, but somehow we've lost our grip on Him. Our faith has grown weak, and our trust has become half-hearted. We are not living by faith in Him.

No wonder Jesus was particularly critical of the Pharisees. They were full of religious activity and they were ceaseless in their concern over Temple matters . . . but they had lost the heart of their faith.

Jesus said,

> 'When judgement day comes, many will say to me, "Lord, Lord, in your Name we spoke God's message, by your name we drove out demons and performed many miracles!" Then I will say to them, "I never knew you. Get away from me, you wicked people."'

If our lives are not entrusted to Jesus, we are none the better. No matter what we do for Him, He still won't know us.

'Who loves me and gives His life for me'

We so easily forget what Jesus is like. We need to see Him again gathering the children around Him, setting them on His knee and blessing them. We need to know again how much He cared about every one of them, and how important they were to Him. We need to visualise Him touching the lepers. Reaching out to the untouchables. Caring for that despised and broken group of people who had no hope and no future. We need to see Him making them whole.

We need to picture Jesus lifting up the paralysed man — and helping him to walk those first halting steps. We need to hear His words of forgiveness, and His promise of healing. And to see Him with the outcasts. The losers, the drop-outs and the poor. The people trapped in a downward spiral of decline. We need to sense His quality of compassion.

If only we could glimpse Him breaking the bread and pouring the wine, and talking of a New Kingdom. Talking of His body broken, and blood shed . . . for love of us.

And if we could see Him hanging on the cross, declaring out of his suffering and heartbreak, 'Father, forgive them,' and granting forgiveness to a dying thief on a cross beside Him.

And wouldn't it be wonderful to see Jesus standing by the Sea of Galilee? And to hear him greeting the downhearted fishermen. Forgiving Peter, the friend who had let Him down.

We need to see Jesus looking at us. To understand that He's been loving us since before we knew His name. To know that He's been beside us through all the good times and the bad, and to understand that He gave His life for us as a sign of just how much He loves us.

As we give Him everything, He gives us Himself. And as His life fills our lives we know a wholeness, a completeness, and a 'rightness' which we never knew before. In His love we find the purpose of our being. In His love we find full salvation.

9: Break Me

The 'Daybreak' musical tour was absolutely exhausting. Every day we travelled to a different town to set up several tons of equipment, rehearsed the local choirs and drama groups, and presented the musical to a packed theatre.

A total of three thousand young people in twenty-eight towns took part, and the total audiences exceeded forty-thousand people. It was an unforgettable experience.

In the production I was Simon Peter. Night after night I had to stand alone on the stage in a blaze of spotlights and react to the stereo-recorded screech of the cock-crow. I had thought a lot about the part, and felt I was really alive to the kind of person that Peter was. Night after night I felt something of the loneliness and defeat of Peter's denial. I entered into Peter's failure as a disciple. The words of that denial scene burnt deep within me.

> 'Call me Peter,
> Misunderstood,
> Call me Peter,
> The rock that moved.
> And I stand by dying embers,
> And I look into the flame.
> And I hear the voice of Jesus,
> And my pride is turned to shame.
> And I hear the piercing cockcrow,
> And the dawn begins to break.
> And I mix with cruel soldiers,
> And I curse and spit and lie,

And I know the mind of Jesus,
And the tears cloud up my eyes.
Call me Peter,
Misunderstood.
Call me Peter,
The rock that moved.'

As the last chords of the last song faded, the de-rig at Southampton Guildhall began. Props, costumes, and loudspeakers were packed, and trundled out into the waiting truck.

The fast 'wrap' at the end of each evening performance was essential if the equipment was to arrive at the next venue in time to be set up next morning. I stood in the chill night air and watched the last pieces of equipment disappear into the van.

I looked up at the Guildhall clock, it was just after midnight. It was my turn to travel overnight in the truck. So I clambered into the cab next to the driver and wrapped my coat around me. It was going to be a very long night. The truck was so full of equipment that the air brakes squealed and hissed each time we went down hill. Then the engine strained and roared as we climbed the next gradient.

The roads were covered with mist. The noise of the engine made conversation impossible; and no matter how I tried I couldn't find a comfortable position for sleep.

Hour after hour we rolled along in this kind of unreal world. My thoughts turned back to the previous evening's performance. The sounds and images of 'Daybreak' rolled around my mind. I remembered Paul Field's 'Denial' song, which ended the cock-crow scene.

'Surely this is stony ground on which to build your kingdom?
Surely, Lord, you might have found a better man than me?
There must be many, Lord, much worthier than I.
There must be many, Lord, more brave.

For I fear that I'm not strong enough to lift your cross on high
There must be many much more worthy, many stronger you could save.

Surely this is cloudy water for turning into wine?
Surely the most sour and bitter, of the grapes upon your vine.
Oh I don't mean to sound ungrateful Lord you know,
But even with the strength we found,
In all your power and wisdom Lord there must be some mistake.
For I am weak Lord, so very weak Lord, and I will only let you down.'

The roar of the engine and the swirling mist before the headlights seemed to cut me off from reality. It was like being in a state of suspended animation. It felt very eerie.

I began to look at my life, and the words of the Peter scene and the Denial song began to haunt me. As my mind back-tracked down the years I began to feel a failure as a disciple of Jesus Christ. I knew that I was a Christian, and that Jesus Christ was my Saviour. But as the miles rolled by I became aware of whole areas of my life that were not really yielded to His Lordship. As I re-traced my own spiritual pilgrimage I saw that I had grown more in love with the work of Christ than with Christ Himself. I needed to offer myself to Him again in a more complete way.

As soon as we arrived in Cornwall early the next morning I found a room and some privacy. I knelt and offered my life back to the One who had given His life for me. In that small room I was broken again before Him. I offered every aspect of my life and ministry back to Him; and my heart overflowed with a new love for Him. It was not the first time that I had done this, neither was it to be the last. It was just another phase in my growing and developing relationship with Jesus Christ.

Jeremiah's vision of the Potter and the clay is very important to me. It expresses something which is at the heart of my own Christian experience — God's ongoing work in shaping my life.

God is the Potter, I am the clay. All my high ideals and bright ideas are of no use or purpose unless I am in the Potter's hand. My life will only be useful if I'm in His will.

Epilogue

Clay Pots

I have been writing this book while on holiday in Wales. Today, I visited a tiny Welsh pottery. Just one lady, working in a wooden shack in a small village called Llanboidy.

I stood and watched her at work. Out of the same batch of clay she made mugs, milk-jugs, plant pots, ovenware and ornaments. She worked quickly and skilfully, lining up the things she'd made on the shelf beside her ready to be fired.

The clay had no say in what it would become. Some of it was used to make ornaments which would be prominently displayed, and the rest for functional use in the kitchen or garden. Each piece of clay took on a different purpose in her hands. Each pot was different. Each item was unique. Each piece of clay became what she intended.

As I watched the potter at work I saw her take a rough piece of clay and make it into something beautiful. So many of us concentrate on what we should *do* for the Lord, the real emphasis should be on what we should *become*.

As we offer our lives over to Him again and again we give Him the opportunity to shape us. To become what He intends us to be . . . beautiful people, with lives full of purpose and meaning that bring glory to Him our Creator.

Only the Potter sees the end from the beginning. Only

He knows what beauty can be shaped from our selfish lives. Only He has the vision of what we might become. Only He can see our full potential, and only He can achieve it in us.

> 'Yet we who have this spiritual treasure are like common clay pots, in order to show that the supreme power belongs to God, not to us. We are often troubled, but not crushed; sometimes in doubt, but never in despair; there are many enemies, but we are never without a friend; and though badly hurt at times, we are not destroyed. At all times we carry in our mortal bodies the death of Jesus, so that His life may be seen in our bodies.'
> St. Paul.

THROUGH DAVID'S PSALMS

Derek Prince

Derek Prince, internationally known Bible teacher and scholar, draws on his understanding of the Hebrew language and culture, and a comprehensive knowledge of Scripture, to present 101 meditations from the Psalms.

Each of these practical and enriching meditations is based on a specific passage and concludes with a faith response. They can be used either for personal meditation or for family devotions. They are intended for all those who want their lives enriched or who seek comfort and encouragement from the Scriptures.

LOVING GOD

Charles Colson

Loving God is the very purpose of the believer's life, the vocation for which he is made. However loving God is not easy and most people have given little real thought to what the greatest commandment really means.

Many books have been written on the individual subjects of repentence, Bible study, prayer, outreach, evangelism, holiness and other elements of the Christian life. In **Loving God**, Charles Colson draws all these elements together to look at the entire process of growing up as a Christian.

Combining vivid illustrations with straightforward exposition he shows how to live out the Christian faith in our daily lives. **Loving God** provides a real challenge to deeper commitment and points the way towards greater maturity.

THE TORN VEIL

Sister Gulshan and Thelma Sangster

Gulshan Fatima was brought up in a Muslim Sayed family according to the orthodox Islamic code of the Shias.

Suffering from a crippling paralysis she travelled to England in search of medical help. Although unsuccessful in medical terms, this trip marked the beginning of a spiritual awakening that led ultimately to her conversion to Christianity.

Gulshan and her father also travelled to Mecca in the hope that God would heal her, but that trip too was of no avail. However, Gulshan was not detered. She relentlessly pursued God and He faithfully answered her prayers. Her conversion, when it came, was dramatic and brought with a miraculous healing.

The Torn Veil is Sister Gulshan's thrilling testimony to the power of God which can break through every barrier.

NOW I CALL HIM BROTHER

Alec Smith

Alec Smith, son of Ian Smith the rebel Prime Minister of Rhodesia whose Unilateral Declaration of Independence plunged his country into twelve years of bloody racial war, has written his own story of those years.

The story of his life takes him from early years of rebellion against his role as 'Ian Smith's son' through his youth as a drop-out, hippy and drug peddler into the Rhodesian forces.

A dramatic Christian conversion experience at the height of the civil war transformed his life and led to the passionate conviction to see reconciliation and peace in a deeply divided country.

What follows is a thrilling account of how God can take a dedicated life and help to change the course of history.